PRAISE FOR *KITCHEN TABLE MAGIC*

"Melissa Cynova breaks down magic in a way that is accessible, doable, and totally inspiring. The first minute you dive in you will feel empowered to live a truly magical life. Buy this book, read it cover to cover, mark it up, fold down the corners of the pages, spill stuff on it, and let Melissa's kitchen table teaching change your life in the best ways possible."

—Madame Pamita, author of *The Book of Candle Magic*

"Brew a cup of tea, sit down, and listen in as Melissa Cynova brings her fresh, modern, and totally hands-on approach to magic in her newest book, *Kitchen Table Magic*. Using ordinary ingredients you find around your house, you'll learn how to cast a spell for love, prosperity, health, and more. There are no complicated instructions, no arcane objects. (Buh-bye eye of newt!) Just simple, everyday magic that anyone can do. Cynova delivers a ton of useful info (and spells that actually work) with a side of her inimitable wit."

—Theresa Reed, author of *The Tarot Coloring Book* and *Astrology for Real Life*

"Welcome back to the table. In *Kitchen Table Magic*, Melissa Cynova reminds us of the magic that is within us all. Remember the vibe, how to tap into it, and start reclaiming your inner magic now. Melissa has written another wonderful guide filled with lessons and stories."

—Jaymi Elford, author of *Tarot Inspired Life*

T0043106

"I loved *Kitchen Table Magic*. Melissa removes stigmas and would-be secrets as to how magic can have an active role in your life in that classic 'discussion over tea' way. There can be a lot of rules and gatekeeping when it comes to initiating a magical practice, which in all honesty becomes overwhelming. Through this book, Melissa remains down to earth and practical by encouraging you that your practice is as unique as you are."

—Jamie Sawyer, artist at SacredSpaceTattoo.com

KITCHEN TABLE
Magic

ABOUT THE AUTHOR

Melissa Cynova (she/her) has been reading tarot cards and making magic since she was a kid. Her first book, *Kitchen Table Tarot,* won the Independent Publishing Award for Best First Book and COVR Visionary awards. Her second book, *Tarot Elements: Five Readings to Reset Your Life,* was released in 2019. *Navigating the Scorpio Sea*, the companion book to Maggie Stiefvater's *Scorpio Sea Tarot,* was released in fall 2020.

Melissa lives in St. Louis with her person, Joe; her lovely teenagers; two dogs; four black cats; and a tortoise named Phil. She is super into 1,000+ piece jigsaw puzzles, superhero movies, and exhaling with her friends.

ALSO BY MELISSA CYNOVA

Kitchen Table Tarot

Tarot Elements

Scorpio Sea Tarot (with Maggie Stiefvater)

FIRST EDITION
Second Printing, 2020

Cover design by Kevin R. Brown
Cover illustration and interior art pieces by Harry Briggs
Interior art by the Llewellyn Art Department
Tarot card descriptions in chapter 12 from *Kitchen Table Tarot* by Melissa Cynova
© 2017 by Llewellyn Worldwide, Ltd. 2143 Wooddale Drive, Woodbury, MN
55125. All rights reserved. Used by permission.

Llewellyn Publications is a registered trademark of Llewellyn Worldwide Ltd.

Library of Congress Cataloging-in-Publication Data
Names: Cynova, Melissa, author.
Title: Kitchen table magic : pull up a chair, light a candle & let's talk
magic / Melissa Cynova.
Description: First edition. | Woodbury, MN : Llewellyn Publications, [2020]
| Includes bibliographical references. | Summary: "A nondenominational
collection of folk magic practices for love, luck, prosperity, protection,
blessings, healing, and goal-setting"— Provided by publisher.
Identifiers: LCCN 2020019111 (print) | LCCN 2020019112 (ebook) | ISBN
9780738762708 (paperback) | ISBN 9780738762982 (ebook)
Subjects: LCSH: Magic.
Classification: LCC BF1611 .C96 2020 (print) | LCC BF1611 (ebook) | DDC
133.4/3—dc23
LC record available at https://lccn.loc.gov/2020019111
LC ebook record available at https://lccn.loc.gov/2020019112

Llewellyn Worldwide Ltd. does not participate in, endorse, or have any authority or responsibility concerning private business transactions between our authors and the public.

All mail addressed to the author is forwarded but the publisher cannot, unless specifically instructed by the author, give out an address or phone number.

Any internet references contained in this work are current at publication time, but the publisher cannot guarantee that a specific location will continue to be maintained. Please refer to the publisher's website for links to authors' websites and other sources.

Llewellyn Publications
A Division of Llewellyn Worldwide Ltd.
2143 Wooddale Drive
Woodbury, MN 55125-2989
www.llewellyn.com

Printed in the United States of America

KITCHEN TABLE
Magic

PULL UP A CHAIR, LIGHT A CANDLE & LET'S TALK MAGIC

MELISSA CYNOVA

Llewellyn Publications
Woodbury, Minnesota

ACKNOWLEDGEMENTS

To Maggie, who showed me how to tell a story on paper instead of in my head.

This book is dedicated to my ancestor, Krystyna Ceynowa, who was the last woman killed in the Polish witch hunts. I hope that she's proud of me. In defiance and love, I honor you.

For every evil under the sun
There is a remedy or there is none.
If there be one, try and find it;
If there be none, never mind it.

—MOTHER GOOSE[1]

---

1. P.S. Mother Goose was totally a witch with her pointed hat and her goose familiar, flying around in her cauldron.

CONTENTS

Introduction

There is nothing about magic that holds it out of your reach. You can't be too poor or too young or too brown or too queer. You can't be unqualified. You can't be in the wrong spiritual tradition, even if your spiritual tradition is none at all. You can't be removed from the magic, because it lives inside of you.

You knew it when you were young, making potions out of rainwater and wild mushrooms. You felt it when you read *Matilda* and Harry Potter and realized that sometimes, if the idea was clear enough and your intent was large enough, you could make things happen too. It's very easy to rationalize those things away. I found myself drawn to any book about magic that I could find—from Mercedes Lackey's Valdemar series to the seemingly magical Encyclopedia Brown, who used logic as his magic wand, and from Meg and Charles Wallace in *A Swiftly Tilting Planet* to Shakespeare's Titania and witches three. I sought them out because I believed in them. I believed in what they could do, and I believed that I could create amazing things too.

My friend Karen Rontowski was talking with me before recording her podcast, *Paranormal Karen*. She offhandedly said, "I'd love to learn magic, but I don't have time to study and go to classes. It seems so formal." I nearly swallowed my gum.

Although I know people who have studied high or ceremonial magic, most of the witches or practitioners I know are "throw some salt at it" kind of folks.

What I mean by this is that I came into magic kind of by accident and never learned the ceremonial way. Most of the women in my life had little magics that they used around the house all the time. Make a handprint star on a seed when you plant it; say a prayer so it grows. Now, they would likely never call it magic, but that's what it is. To bless a plant, to remove negative energy, to look at the leaves to see if they've flipped over and are waiting for rain. This is the magic we all know. This is the magic that's part of our heritage. This is a collection of folk magic and Neopaganism that does not prescribe to any specific faith tradition. The faith is all you.

I have been practicing magic since before I knew what magic really was. My favorite book when I was young was called *The Girl with the Silver Eyes*, about a girl named Katie who was special and had to figure out how to use her powers. I felt I had so much in common with her. I knew that there was something amazing about me and in me, but I couldn't figure out what it was.

It took finding other witches and books for me to figure it out. I finally could name what I was: *witch*. I could finally name what I could do: *magic*. There have been times when I've forgotten that I'm a witch, when the universe or circumstance knocked the wind out of me, but I've always come back to it, this control over the world around me, of myself, of my intentions. This is my gift. This is what I was trying to figure out as a child. It's been over twenty years now since I was finally able to name it, and it grows stronger every year.

In this book, I will use the words *witch* and *magic*. Magic is the energy you possess to control your life. A witch, to me, is anyone who has and uses magic. It does not rely on gender or magical studies. Being a witch and using magic are not exclusive to any faith, belief system, or religion. Witchcraft and magic are inherent. Intuition and psychic energy are the same; they just come from different directions. Intuition comes from the inside, and psychic energy comes from the outside. Therefore, spirituality and religion are not necessary. They're welcome if you want them to be, but they are not at all necessary. Your magic can be added to your spiritual tradition, or you can keep it separate. It's up to you.

I believe that the name and power have been diminished and mocked. Reclaiming this power is a wonderful way to stand a little taller, have more self-reliance, and honor those ancestors we've lost. If you want to learn magic with ease and a little bit of sass, this is the book for you. It's intent paired with your surroundings. It's a knowing of the old ways and how to make them your own. This is a magic starter kit.

To begin, let's do a little spell together. All that you need is a pen and paper. Think of something you want. A new book, some money, help quitting a bad habit. Let's say it's for your new boss to listen to you when you're in a meeting. Super easy. We're going to write what's called a petition in the simplest way possible: on a sticky note.

Write the words "I am a valuable member of this team. Hear me." Write them over and over until you run out of room on the note. Fold it in thirds and then in thirds again the other way. Take this little note and tuck it away somewhere in your house.

The next time you have a meeting, remember this note and re-member that you've decided that you'll be heard. Watch what happens.

This spell is exactly what I'm talking about. You see a situation in which the power has been taken from you—or was never given to you. You decide to do something about it, and then you put your will into the universe and make it so. There is power here.

This quote in the novel *Boy's Life* by author Robert McCam-mon is essentially the thesis statement for this book: "We all start out knowing magic. We are born with whirlwinds, forest fires, and comets inside us. We are born able to sing to birds and read the clouds and see our destiny in grains of sand."[1]

Think about when you were little how accessible magic was to you. I remember mixing rainwater, plants, and seeds and call-ing it a potion. I would put bright yellow dandelions in the po-tion for happiness and ground-up acorns if I felt small. I would make the potion match what I needed and choose the ingredi-ents as I wanted. I mixed them together and used the words that matched my feelings. In that blur of childhood sunshine, I hon-estly can't remember if they worked, but I do remember that they made me feel better. I felt as if I had some control over my life. Little kids are tossed about a lot by other people's agendas and needs. I clearly remember my spell crafting being a bright light of control for me.

I would draw circles around me with my finger and declare that I was safe. And I *felt* safe. With puberty, though, came a huge onrushing of "You don't belong" that knocked the breath out of me. My magics became smaller and then disappeared. I was no longer confident that I could think my way to happiness.

---

1. Robert McCammon, *Boy's Life* (New York: Simon & Schuster, 1991), 2.

McCammon continues to share all the words that I sought throughout my life. He wrote, "But then we get the magic educated right out of our souls. We get it churched out, spanked out, washed out, and combed out. We get put on the straight and narrow and told to be responsible. Told to act our age. Told to grow up, for God's sake. And you know why we were told that? Because people doing the telling were afraid of our wildness and youth, and because the magic we knew made them ashamed and sad of what they'd allowed to wither in themselves."[2]

Luckily, I grew out of that slump. You go through this period of development, and possibly some tragedy, and on the other side of it, you don't really recognize yourself. I was not the same girl who went to Catholic school and believed what I was told. I was not a child who could spin fantasies into magical places to be safe. I wasn't a girl who could white knuckle her way through hard situations. I was a woman and was confused and needed direction. I looked for that direction in alcohol and other people, in turning my brain off and spending hours playing video games. None of this filled the time properly, though. Nothing could compete with finding confidence in myself. Nothing could compete with this nagging feeling that I could be in charge of my life. I suspected it. I thought that something was wrong and that I was stronger than I was behaving, but it took me a while to figure out what it was that needed to be fixed.

It was magic. I needed to recognize and use my magic.

Before you think that I stayed in this Wonder Woman, badass place, I frequently forget that I can use magic, and on occasion I flounder around foolishly, complaining that things aren't going right in my life. It happens less frequently than it used to, but it still

2. McCammon, *Boy's Life*, 2.

happens. Sometimes it's easier to allow yourself to be powerless and morph into a Muggle for a while. It's okay. But sooner or later, your magic will wake you up again to the possibilities of a life that you are driving.

For the most part, I've reclaimed the power that I was born with and started working actively to improve my own life. I found my focus—and my passion. I found like-minded witchy folks and exchanged ideas and spells with them. I started wearing a pentacle every day, but only recently outside of my shirt. (I do live in the Midwest.) A psychic once told me that in this lifetime, I was going to gather my fellow witches from lives past. Come together, then, brothers and sisters and siblings all. Come together and learn how strong you can be.

This book is going to help you get started with your magical journey. You'll learn to listen to yourself, how to best use the supplies available to you, and how to focus your energy. You'll learn to follow the moon and your own intuition. You'll learn about magic on a dime and how to make your resources work for you. We'll talk about the psychology of magic, the traditions and the new twists on tradition, and honoring ancestors and guides. This is your birthright, no matter where you were born. This is a re-learning of the gift already given to you.

I saved you a seat at my kitchen table. Grab some tea and get comfy. We're going to be here for a while.

XO,
Melissa

PART ONE

The Basics

CHAPTER 1

What Is Magic?

Magic is the place that exists between what we know and what we don't know. Think of the development of science in the past few hundred years. We used to think that thunder and lightning were the gods' expressions of emotion. We used to think that anything we couldn't understand was magic. As science stepped up, magic receded a bit, but it's still there. Sometimes I have dreams that come true. How do we explain that? There has been some research into the prefrontal cortex, and it might be related to dreaming and precognition. But we don't *know* that.

I've done tarot readings for over thirty years and have given some amazingly accurate readings to strangers. I have been able to see when they would become well, when they would get a job, how their marriage would go. How, though? I have no idea. The only proof that I have is a mountain of anecdotal evidence.

I have given readings to folks that have begun with me looking at the cards and saying, "So if you're not happy in your marriage, you have some decisions to make," causing the person to start crying and ask me how I knew that. And call me creepy. I don't have an answer for their question. I don't know how I do this. I just know that it works and that the more confidence I have in my readings, the more accurate they are.

The same is true with magic.

My friend Jane called me in tears. She was poly and was dating a few people. A new person she was talking to said that they'd heard terrible things about her from one of her ex-partners, and because of this, they didn't want to date her. The rumors were untrue, cruel, and energetically sticky. She tried to have a conversation with the ex-partner, but they were shutting her out. She tried to talk to the new person and tell them it wasn't true, but they didn't listen.

Jane was exhausted. She said she felt like she had tar on her and couldn't get it off. I invited two other friends to come over, one witch and one reiki master. As soon as Jane came over, we felt what was going on energetically. It *felt* like she had tar all over her. Her movements were slow, she was deeply sad, and we could sense it. I love her, and I didn't want to hug her.

I'd asked her to take a shower before she came over, so she was clean. We started by lighting candles around us in a circle. I used a cedar and sage stick to clear the energy in the circle and then the energy of the two friends who came to help, making certain to clean our hands, since those were the tools we were going to use to get this energetic funk off Jane. We started at her head and pulled away things that we could *feel* sticking to her. We sent the gunk into the candles to burn up. We worked from the top of her head to her feet. Her heart was the hardest part to clean. At one point, our reiki friend just held her hand over Jane's heart and we all had a good cry. After she was cleaned energetically, we draped her in a blanket, fed her, and told her how much we loved her. And then she slept so hard. The next day, she said she felt like a weight had lifted off her and all the connections to the poisonous people were severed.

This was magic.

Blues singer Robert Johnson was a masterful guitar player. It was said that he had little skill, then disappeared for a while and came back playing songs that were truly mind-blowing. Because of this, it was said—maybe because it was true—that he sold his soul to the devil at a crossroads in Mississippi.

My husband and I were planning a trip to New Orleans that would take us through Mississippi and right past two places that were said to be *the* crossroads where Mr. Johnson sold his soul. I mean, we had to go, right? We timed it so we would arrive at midnight, because we were either super brave or super stupid.

We got to the "official" crossroads, which had a hokey neon sign and zero energy in it. Nothing. It felt like a gas station. We started off to the "unofficial" crossroads, and things got interesting really quickly. I felt like I was completely exposed to the energy and like I was being watched. Not being watched like you're in a restaurant and someone is trying to figure out who you are—*being watched* like someone has seen you, has taken note of you, and has intent toward you. Creepy as hell. We got out so Joe could take a few pictures, and the feeling intensified. I felt like not only were we being watched, but like we were trespassing. I heard this very subtle sound in my head that got a little louder the longer we stayed: get out, *get out*, GET OUT GET OUT. So we got out of there. We started driving away and were both spooked. Joe didn't hear anything, but as we drove over a creek (running water), he shuddered. He said, "Something was holding on to me, honey. I could feel it. It was stuck on the small of my back. It felt like I was being pulled like a thread from a sweater. When we went over the creek, it snapped free."

Joe didn't know that running water stops magic in its tracks. He didn't know that things could come along for a ride if you were too open energetically. He didn't know that crossroads were super powerful magical places—it's where you make agreements with the other side. What he did know was that something had touched him, held on to him, and then lost its grip.

This is magic too.

After a particularly terrible year, in which I felt like nothing could go right and people I loved kept dying, I was feeling awfully low. One of our New Year traditions is to make a vision board and burn the one from the previous year. I'd decided that I was going to leave all that heartache and anxiety behind me and burned my old vision board in our firepit. I watched it burn and imagined all the hurt and pain lessening. I imagined all the downfalls and heartaches fading away. I imagined that I could be a phoenix and come out of the ashes with renewed purpose.

As I did this, I felt a weight lift off my shoulders. I don't think that expression is an accident. I literally felt something fall off of me. After the last of the vision board burned away, I felt about fifty pounds lighter and felt actually happy for the first time in months. There was no other reason for this other than meditation by a fire and a clear decision to leave my past in the past. The new year *was* better, and I wasn't slowed by the ghosts of crappy years past. Because of this, the future *felt* brighter, so I was better able to move into it undeterred.

This is magic too.

There are a few things to discuss when it comes to the kinds of magic there are. We're going to talk about folk magic, American magic, and magical communities. I wanted to spend some time here for a few reasons. I think that folk magic is highly underrated and unnoticed, and there are some cultural reasons for that, which should be examined.

In the American magic section, I'll talk about how hard it is to figure out what is Appalachian magic versus Ozark magic versus Hoodoo. Our little country has its problems to be sure, but what we share is greater than what we don't. Most of our pasts, as diverse as they are, have mingled at some point. We've picked up cultural and magical traditions from each other and shared the ways that work. This book was originally going to be a cultural look at magic. Irish, Polish, West Indian, African, Gullah—I was going to share spells and ideas from all over our beautiful country. The problem was, I couldn't. There are some regional notations here and there, but for the most part, magic is magic. This was frustrating and delightful to find, and I am embracing the idea that there are more things we all have in common than there are things that separate us.

That said, there is nothing wrong with seeking a magical community in which you feel comfortable. There are groups of root witches, hedge witches, Heathens, priestesses of Brigid, and diverse groups of Pagans whose shared belief in nature and magic bring them together. If you feel that your magic would be better as a shared experience, there is no end to the communities and groups that are out there for you.

FOLK MAGIC

When you ask someone what folk magic is, they usually speak first about their grandparents or great-grandparents. You hear stories about red strings being tied around the legs of furniture by someone's nonna, but it was never talked about. It just existed. Why do your aunties whisper the word *cancer*? Why do they lift their feet when they drive over railroad tracks?

Folk magic lives in superstition and in tradition. It's closely connected to the earth around us and the region in which it was created. It's connected to the elements around us and the ways that we can reach out and become a part of them. It is not, of course, exclusively the realm of traditional feminine folks. Masculine folks live here too, but it's been consigned to this area. Assigned, even. Women's magic. It's a thing. For my purposes, I'm not a big fan of gendering the universe, so let's just call it folk magic and be done.

This is the magic of the everyday. This is as common as housekeeping and as routine as washing the sheets. This is maintenance of magic that helps your life align with your best self. From buying a new broom when you move so that you don't bring old dirt into your new house, to using a salt jar to protect yourself from negative energy. This is magic that you can do daily and incorporate into your life so that everything is ritual. Everything is protected and everything has meaning.

Folk magic is magic of the people, just as folk art is the art of the people. There is some serious classism, racism, and sexism dancing around these distinctions, and that's important to talk about. Ceremonial magic in itself is not a bad thing. It has a history in some practices, however, that should be discussed and analyzed.

Folk art is distinguished from high art because it was mostly the purview of indigenous folks and the poor. It is not "less than." Folk magic is far and away from the ceremonial magic taught mostly by old men. This is not to say that there is no value in learning all of it, but part of the value is in seeing our history for what it is. As a friend said, "Men carry the history and women carry the culture."

Another thing that folk traditions have in common is that they are generally seen as women's business. Men made high art and magic, and women were weaving, embroidering, potting, and sculpting. They were delivering babies and helping folks put their lives into right relations. Women's work has always been seen as more organic, more natural. In less kind terms, it's seen as less than.

Who created the museums that held the art? Who were the patrons of the artists? Who could afford and was allowed into these schools? In order to understand the difference between fine art and folk art, you have to understand the difference between the rich and the poor and the cultural divide that this has caused. This is the same distinction between high magic and folk magic.

My friends remember their grandmothers tying a red string to the baby's crib to keep away the bad spirits. I have an absolute freak out if someone opens an umbrella in the house. Both of these are superstitions/folk magic, and both of them hold power if we believe in them. You can see kids making St. Brigid's crosses every spring, a practice that goes way, way back to Celtic Paganism. You can see the holly and the ivy hung at Christmas celebrations, also an old Pagan tradition. You can find traditional folk magic in the way that people sweep their floors (clockwise) and use Florida water or brick dust to clean their front porches. You can watch someone spill salt and then, quick as thinking, toss some over their shoulder.

You can see patterns in weaving and sewing that are as old as the arts themselves, particularly in the bead and sewing work of some Native American tribes, but also in English basket weaving, Indian architectural styles, and Ghanaian kente cloth. These patterns and designs are inherently magical, and the continuance of their use is no accident. They *mean* something. They have *always* meant something.

ETHICS IN MAGIC

Folk magic has become trendy like the artwork that shows up on backpacks and at Coachella. This is both good and bad, as the line between cultural appropriation and cultural appreciation is a thin, wavering thing. The good part is that the appreciation of native cultures and art will help ensure that it lives beyond private collections and museums. The bad part is that appropriation takes from the culture without giving anything back, much less the respect it deserves.

A good rule of thumb is if you would say, do, or wear the thing in front of the person whose culture created it, it's appreciation. If you would be terribly embarrassed to wear a sombrero and fake Pancho Villa moustache in front of a person of Mexican descent, take the hat off, man. Lose the 'stache.

Taking the art and magic of indigenous folks and presenting it as your own is problematic. Getting a "tribal" tattoo without knowledge and understanding of what that even means is foolish.

When I started working on this book, I wanted to be 100 percent certain that I landed on the cultural appreciation side of this line. You will find practices from European, Native American, Appalachian, Ozark, Mexican, Hoodoo, Pan-African, and South American traditions, representing a lovely mix of all of us. I wanted to put together a distinctly American collection of magic. Not in the red state, blue state idea of America, but in the true spirit of my country, in which all of us together make this rich tapestry beautiful. I have credited the traditions and spells to specific cultures as best as I am able and to the research books where the information was found. If the spell came from my memories or from conversations with friends, I've left them uncredited, as these are part of our collective consciousness. If you see something that is uncredited and you know that it is from a distinct tradition, let me know! I'll put it in the next printing.

AMERICAN MAGIC

For all its problems, America has always had this tapestry thing going on. We've always borrowed from each other and from wherever our families originated. My family is English, Native American, and Polish, predominantly, yet I have a vast knowledge of little magics from all over the world. At the root of magic is a connection to the ground under our feet, the air in our lungs, the spark of life that feeds us, and the blood that flows through our veins. That connection transcends man-made boundaries and arbitrary separations. It gives us a common thread of connectivity that weaves our lives together. All of us feel this connection, and all of us could use a little luck now and again—regardless of the origin of that little magic.

In this book, I don't address any specific religion in the spells and meditation. The reason for this is that I don't think that magic is exclusive to one form of belief. I think that magic is inherent. I think that it can be used within any form of organized (or unorganized) religion and can be utilized outside of religion as well. I believe that it's like thinking. This is a skill that we were born with, and the more we learn and practice, the stronger and better it becomes. Just like intuition, the more you use it, the better it will be. Magic is a combination of your intent, your intuition, and your will.

There are a wide variety of modern magic practitioners. You'll find witches, Heathens, Wiccans, Feri, Reclaiming Pagans, Satanists, Christian magicians, Hoodoo practitioners, Vodouisants, rootworkers, kitchen witches, hedge witches, chaos magicians, Strega, Neoshamans, and feminist witches, as well as magical traditions in nearly every culture and religion.

Imported, recovered, or rebuilt magic from past communities is a rising practice in many communities. Just as Polish me has started studying Polish magic, other folks are reclaiming their magical heritage. There is strength in connecting to your roots and a natural feel and "rightness" that comes from celebrating your ancestors.

I encourage you to use this book as a starting point to your magical studies. Learning more about the practices of others, especially marginalized communities and their magical ways, can only enhance your own practice and empathy.

MAGICAL COMMUNITIES

There are dozens of magical communities out there. With the internet, you can easily find some folks who align with you ethically, magically, and spiritually. I like meet-up websites for finding them. They tend to be less insular than social media groups, and you can see what people really think of the experience.

Pagan, by the way, is a catchall word. It essentially means anything that is pre-Christian, pre-Jewish, and pre-Islamic. Indigenous faith practices are included in this, as well as folks who practice the "old ways" of Nordic, Polish, Romanian, Russian, Irish—you name it—magic.

One of the groups that I'm absolutely enchanted with is a group of Pagans called Heathens. They study and practice Norse religion, with magic as an integral part of that experience. The ones that I've met have had a great deal of integrity and practice the values that they preach. Because they mean what they say—and because integrity is such a strong part of their practice—they are some of the strongest practitioners that I've encountered.

You can find Pagan groups without a specific focus. In St. Louis, we have several that are nature-based, but their practitioners vary from Gardnerian to Wiccan to Druid. They come together to worship at the cycles of the moon and the season, but their personal practices vary when they're at home. There are eco-Pagans and eco-magicians, who focus on the healing of the earth, and groups who worship the old gods in their practice. There are Christian witches and magic practitioners in Islam and Judaism. There are Unitarian Universalists who practice Paganism and Catholic nuns who read tarot cards. The world is full of folks and communities that you can discover and that can add to your magical practice.

With every group, though, comes some danger. I know of groups who prey on newcomers and take advantage of them financially, sexually, and pretty much in any other way you can imagine. Some groups appear to welcome all but are completely transphobic. Some state that they're for the empowerment of men but hold beliefs that put women at risk for sexual predation. As with everything in your life, use your intuition and back it up with some research before you join a magical community. Anything especially shrouded in mystery and "tests" should make you cautious. Speak to people who are in the organization *and* people who have left. Use the internet. Meet in public places. Be sure that the folks that you're meeting with are reputable and do some research about grooming new members that will help you be aware of the warning signs.

Now that you've done your research, you're ready to join a magical community and feel safe and confident. I would recommend first finding out what your moral compass says. There are online tests with questions that help align you with the world's religions; one is called the Belief-O-Matic.[3] After you take these quizzes, you'll have a clearer idea of what is important to you. Human rights? Protection of queer folks? Nonviolence? What is it that motivates you morally?

Whatever it is, these values have to be part of your spiritual community. If you enter a magical group that is misaligned with your morals, you will run into problems down the road. Be an observer for a while. Ask questions. Take notes. Get to know folks before committing any money or other obligations.

I have always been a solitary practitioner, but I have some friends who come together with me when things get troublesome. It's made me lonely for a deeper spiritual connection and community, so I joined a church. I practice my magic alone and occasionally with friends, and I have a spiritual community that is entirely separate. This works beautifully for me. Find what works for you.

I tend to pull together with a few friends on a full or new moon. It has always happened "accidentally." I'll be near their houses and text, "Hey, I'm having breakfast at Morning Glory—you free?" Twenty minutes later, the four of us are drinking coffee, talking about our lives, and supporting each other. And generally laughing our asses off. We head off for one of our houses, and the conversations continue through lunch. One of us will have a new stone to share. One of us will light a candle. We'll share each other's burdens, lean into each other. Be vulnerable in that space. Feed ourselves physically and spiritually. We hug

---

3. You can take Beliefnet's Belief-O-Matic quiz here: https://www.beliefnet .com/entertainment/quizzes/beliefomatic.aspx.

each other and love each other, and we walk away in the late afternoon feeling truly blessed and secure.

This could be called a coven meeting, but since we don't officially call ourselves a coven, it could just be a hang with magic in it. Whatever it is, it strengthens our bonds and makes us all feel better.

When you find a community that makes you feel like this, you'll be home.

Magic is what you need it to be. It's a tool. It's a feeling. It's power. It's calm and it's fury. Magic comes from within and connects with tools, nature, and folks that are in your space. Magic is yours and is defined and used by you: your thoughts, your words, your actions. Your magic.

CHAPTER 2

Getting Started

Margot Adler, NPR journalist and Wiccan priestess, writes in *Drawing Down the Moon,* "Magic is a convenient word for a whole collection of techniques, all of which involve the mind … the mobilization of confidence, will, and emotion brought about by the recognition of necessity."[4] She further points to visualization as the most important technique. Using your mind to manage your body, your mind, and your future is powerful and achievable.

In my experience, there are three stages to magic. The first is *belief.* You believe that your life should be different. You believe that change is possible. If you don't believe in what you're doing, it's not worth doing. The most important part of belief is something that Terry Pratchett (may he rest in riotous peace) called "headology" in several of his Discworld books. This is the practice of speaking and thinking things into truth. Headology holds that things are true because you think they are.

---

4. Margot Adler, *Drawing Down the Moon* (New York: Viking Press, 1979), 8.

The second stage is *words*. They're called spells for a reason, guys. Words matter. If you don't believe me, try to remember the last time someone called you by the wrong name. (Did he call me Michelle? What the hell!?) That's a lot of rage for a slip of the tongue, but they misused the thing that defines you to most of the world—your *word*. Naming is important. Words have power.

The third stage is *action*: you must actually *do* things on the material plane with your meat-sack body in order to make change happen. It's good to light the candle and write the words, but then you must make actual changes to how you live in order to move the universe in the direction you're aiming. Put some good into the world with your actions and look forward to the blessings that will head your way. Action doesn't have to align with your magic but should be in the spirit of it. If you're asking the universe for money, donate what you can. Volunteer. Listen to a friend who's having a hard time. It's hard to be impatient when you're busy helping someone else.

These three stages align beautifully with the tenets of Zoroastrianism: *humata, hukhta, huvarshta*, which mean good thoughts, good words, and good deeds. First you get your head in the right place, then you align your will, and then your actions complete the process. Aligning yourself in mind, body, and spirit is a powerful way to start controlling yourself and your world.

Understand that magic isn't just one thing. It isn't just saying the words or lighting a candle. It's an intentional process that has a beginning, a middle, and an end. You've got to be all in for it to have an effect or any kind of a meaning.

BELIEF

In *Even Cowgirls Get the Blues,* Tom Robbins writes, "I believe in everything, nothing is sacred. I believe in nothing, everything is sacred."[5]

You can change your words around here. Belief can be replaced by faith, sacred attention, intent, prayer, attention, or attitude. It can even be as casual as an assumption or a hunch. For practical purposes, I will use the word *belief.* You can't do magic unless you believe that it will work. At all. Ever. Belief is the spark that carries your needs and hopes to manifestation. Belief is the vehicle. It carries your wish to completion.

Here is an example of how belief can affect your life in ways you couldn't even have imagined. I had a pretty down period a few years ago. During this time, I used to think "That's why I can't have nice things" all the time. *All* the time. It had become a self-deprecating escape for me whenever I screwed something up. I could blame it on me, make it seem like that's the only kind of thing I was capable of, and then deflect any well-meaning constructive criticism or self-inflicted shame. I thought of it as if it were a joke, but it really wasn't funny.

At the same time, things were not good. I was sick a lot. I was unhappy in life, in my job, in my relationships. I couldn't seem to pick my energy up off the floor. I know now that my life was at a low vibration and that I was perpetuating that low vibration by insisting in my head, out loud, to the universe and to anyone who would listen that "I can't have nice things." And even more than that, I decided that my constant screwups were *why* "I couldn't have nice things." I put that in quotes now so I can

5. Tom Robbins, *Even Cowgirls Get the Blues* (New York: Bantam Dell, 1976), 238.

separate it from myself. Do you know why? Because for a long, long time—

I BELIEVED IT.

I consistently and intently stated to God or the universe *and myself* that I was not worthy of those things that I desperately needed.

I thought it with intent.

I thought it with frequency.

I said it out loud.

I said it to friends.

I said it to strangers at the checkout.

I thought it so often that I started to *believe it.*

With my thoughts, I planted the seeds of "I am not worthy." With my words, every time I repeated them, I watered those seeds. With my deeds, I assured the lack of change because I did nothing to shift it.

I am not saying that thinking and saying this was the cause of my unhappiness. It didn't cause me to get a divorce or take a terrible job. This thought didn't keep me from moving forward in my life. What it did was deliver my wish (to not deserve) into manifestation. I was doing magic and I didn't even realize it. I was putting a clear expectation out into the universe and then accepting it as a matter of fact. Of course things were bad—I expected it. I was comfortable in it. I created and invested in that low vibration and did nothing to try to change it.

I set a condition in my life that unhappiness was acceptable. I'd resigned myself for a less-than life, and after a while, I didn't think that there was anything wrong with it. I got used to being unhappy, and whenever I screwed up, I repeated the thought that I didn't deserve happiness in the first place. I set my goals so low that I couldn't even see them anymore.

I am very fortunate that my friend Mark heard me say this one time and said, "Have you ever thought that the reason you can't have nice things is because you actually believe that and keep saying it?" Ouch. Not only was this super painful to hear, but it's a great example of why magical communities can work when they're done right. I never heard myself say this, not really. But Mark did.

Super accurate things tend to sting the most and stick in your brain the longest. I couldn't put this thought down. My belief in this idea and repetition of the self-deprecating mantra created a spell. My repetition of this spell over and over helped me perpetuate the low vibration that I found myself in.

Belief, in this instance, is not just hope. It's not wishing that things were different. It's seeing the change that you need to make in the world *so clearly* that not changing doesn't make sense anymore. When you drive a car, you're supposed to look at the spot that you're about to be in. You don't look at the ditch or the car that's three spots up. You don't look at the narrow shoulders or the guy who's tailgating you. You look at the road ahead, always. If you look to the side, you'll unconsciously make decisions to drive in that direction. If there is a ditch ahead, you keep watching the road that you're on, because you will absolutely err on the side of the ditch, and that's not good for anyone.

This was put into practice one time while I was driving and saw a group of deer over to the side of the road. It was all I could think about. What if they started running into the road? What is the impact of a big-ass deer on a 2006 Corolla? Before I knew it, I'd drifted onto the rumble strip on the road, and had to pull my car back onto the highway. The deer? The deer were fine. They didn't come onto the road and didn't give a fig about the fact that my dad was now glaring at me from the passenger's seat, saying,

"Took your eyes off the road, huh? How'd that work out for you?" Goddamnit. Stupid deer.

Amy Cuddy published studies about and popularized the "power position," standing with your hands on your hips, like Wonder Woman. This has been proven to decrease your cortisol levels and increase your testosterone levels. When these levels shift, your confidence grows by around 25 percent.[6] This is headology. Maybe you're not feeling particularly confident. Maybe you've had a trash can day and you have a challenging meeting ahead of you. Just standing in this confident pose for two minutes can shift your approach to whatever comes next. It doesn't mean that your day was less bad. It just equips you with the framework of confidence so that you can, in a sense, fake it till you make it.

It's the same as putting on makeup when you don't feel well. You are presenting a certain way to the world and your energy can rise up to meet the expectation of a bright-eyed, fully present human being. A favorite pair of jeans, some good stompy boots—whatever it is that pushes your physical and emotional self forward while your brain catches up to the rest of you.

In these two scenarios, using the power pose and the "fake it till you make it wishful eyeliner," you are placing your belief and your body ahead of the present. You are casting energy into the future, certain that imitating confidence will relay that confidence to your soul and you won't sink into the background in that meeting. You put on makeup like armor and trust that it will deflect anything that comes at you that will see you as less than.

6. Dana R. Carney, Amy J. C. Cuddy, and Andy J. Wap, "Power Posing: Brief Nonverbal Displays Affect Neuroendocrine Levels and Risk Tolerance," *Psychological Science* 21, no. 10 (2010): 1363–68, doi:10.1177/0956797610383437.

Belief becomes knowing, then visualization becomes seeing. When you use visualization, you feel more prepared when the moment of transformation occurs. You've already practiced it a million times. I know what my future house looks like because I've imagined it so many times. I know what color my office will be and how the backyard is shaped. I have seen this very clearly in my mind so that when I see it for the first time, I'll recognize it as home.

Imagine a difficult day at work. Maybe you leave a meeting that was frustrating, was pointless, and didn't even have food. You go back to your desk frustrated and feeling a bit defeated. Instead of going straight back to the computer screen, close your eyes. Imagine all those concerns and worries as gray balloons floating above you. They're tied with gray strings all along your arms. Name each one of them. Then imagine that they become untied. One by one, they float off you and head to the ceiling, out the window. Imagine that they're dissolving in the light. Lift your chin. Take a deep breath. Now you can get back to work.

That's what headology is. That's what belief does. It shows you the framework of what could be so clearly that you have no hesitation about stepping into it.

WORDS

What happens when you sprinkle a handful of seeds on the ground? Even if you don't tend to them, even if you don't encourage their growth, they grow. They are tenacious things, seeds. Their whole job is to figure out how to grow, how to find some earth, some water, and some space. They're built for it.

It's the same with words. Words that we say out loud or carry in our hearts. These words are seeds, and they grow if you let them. Think about this. Every chance I could deflect attention away from the mess my life had become, I insisted *forcefully* that this behavior that I could control and was in charge of was actually out of my control and out of the realm of possibility. I was not able, capable, willing, or deserving of good things. Of good people, good security, good home, good job.

One time, I had a driver who was a conspiracy theorist. I absolutely loved this guy. He drove me from Upstate New York to the airport. John spent our hour-long drive telling me the truth about the universe, from the Kennedy assassination to the moon landing. One of the many, many things that he said to me was this: "Catholics will always be happy with being middle class or lower because they chant every week, 'Lord, I am not worthy to receive you, but only say the word and I shall be healed.' They say it so often that they believe it, and they accept their place in life."

Whoa.

First of all, very astute, John. I grew up Catholic and said this sentence every week for decades. I never *thought* about it before, though. This sentence comes from Matthew 8:8 in the Christian Bible. Before a person welcomes Jesus into their house, they say, "Lord, I am not worthy that you should come under my roof: but speak the word only, and my servant shall be healed."[7]

The purpose of this is to acknowledge that every human is flawed and that we are not worthy enough for God to interact with us on an intimate level. In a Catholic mass, the words are said before the congregants take the Eucharist, which is a ritual symbolizing taking the body and blood of Christ into you. It's the most important part of the mass.

I truly mean no disrespect to Catholics when I ask this, but I need to know: Why do I have to tear myself down to be close

7. King James 2000 Bible.

to God? Actually, I don't need to know, because I left the church, but it's worth thinking about—a group of people chanting "I am not worthy to receive you" in unison, week after week, with intent and passion as part of a ritualized religious practice in a house of God.

That's not nothin', you guys. I think John was on to something.

Words have power. Names have more power. Calling something what it is defines it and defines your relationship with that thing. I had a friend who had problems with concentration his whole life. At thirty-two, he was diagnosed with pretty severe ADD. Once he could put a name to it, he was once again in charge of his life. Once named, his distractions lost their influence and became identifiable obstacles that he could direct and control. He could seek appropriate counseling and medication and call his "distractions" what they really were: symptoms. Knowing the name—what words to use for something—tells you where you are in relation to it and how to best kick its ass.

If you're doing a prosperity spell, an important part of that is visualizing yourself in that space. Not worried about bills, not owing anyone anything. Having a better car. Not having to play bill roulette for a while. If this part stays an aspiration, it makes the magic difficult. If you can't see what you need, how are you meant to realize it? If you constantly see yourself as poor, rising above that is going to be a lot more difficult. If you can shift your mind to align with your new reality, however, it'll be like putting on an old jacket that fits just right. *Then*, when you have your mind right, you can find the proper words to bind them with.

ACTION

In correspondence with Bill Wilson regarding the creation of Alcoholics Anonymous, Carl Jung wrote, "You are what you do, not what you say you'll do."[8] There is magical action and mundane (Muggle) action. Both are important. The first part is the magical part.

The practical parts of a spell are the items that you use to push forth your vision. Write your intent or sigils. Use earth, air, fire, and water to symbolically charge your intention.

Intent is everything.

You have to mean this. That's the spark that gets the fire of action going. You know what it is to want something, but do you know what it is to mean it? To feel the resolution of a decision? To have those embers of determination pushing you forward, even when it hurts? Even when it's hard? Even when you don't think you can anymore, that small light of resolve carries you through. It's what makes you finish writing your book when it's 3:30 in the morning and you're just so tired. It's what makes you fiercely devoted to those that you love. That intention will pull you through when you don't see the end of the path.

While many witches (including myself) use special tools, you don't need them. You should know that if you are unable to access them for any reason, it's okay. You can do the work without the tools. Lack of accessibility to items should not keep you from doing magic. In fact, nothing should get in the way of your magic. You don't need tools. They help, but they're not a requirement. All you need is your thoughts. Your words. Your deeds. You clear the air around you, find some quiet, and create a workplace for your magic. It's a deliberate act that points all your resources in the same direction.

---

8. Ian McCabe, *Carl Jung and Alcoholics Anonymous* (London: Routledge, 2015).

I learned how to do tarot readings without any one-on-one coaching. I remember reading in a friend's living room, apologizing for still needing to use my book, agonizing over every card meaning that I came across, and being absolutely shocked that the reading was not only correct but also nuanced and far beyond any insight that I brought to the situation naturally. I remember reading in the back of cars on the way to concerts. At bars that were so loud and bright that I had to shout the reading to the (usually drunk) client. I did this for years. I read when I was exhausted, drunk, high, emotionally fraught, and sad. I read through all of that, because I didn't know any better. I didn't know that if I was emotionally, spiritually, physically, and psychically grounded, the reading would be second nature. I didn't know that there were ways to make my readings effortless. I learned the hard way, and it wasn't until later in my life that I learned that meditation, incense, candles, and crystals could help me make the reading easier, just as with magic.

I have memories of trying and trying to make something magical happen. Reaching out with heartbreak to the universe and being met with silence. Lighting a candle and watching it burn down, not doing any actions to help the candle do its job. Wishing with all my might that something would happen and not seeing any results. It's frustrating to do things the hard way. The results are rarely what we want them to be when we do half the work that's needed. The magic exists inside you, and the candles and crystals just help clarify the signal you're trying to send to the universe and give it some more pop.

I think that understanding why these traditions work is an important part of using them. I never noticed until I was an adult that in a Catholic mass, the bell was rung by the altar boys during the most sacred part of the mass. The job of the bell wasn't arbitrary at all. Its job was to draw everyone's attention to the front of the church at that precise time.

Chanting helps you get into a meditative space. Any chant outside of a soccer stadium will get to a place where each line sounds the same every time you say it. It will maintain chill tones and will drop you into your quiet space. If you choose to work with others, it will get you all into the same space at the same time.

Repeating a prayer or spell helps you visualize and manifest it. This is different from chanting because this is not always aloud. If you write, "I will get this job. I will get this job. I will get this job," that idea will become burned into your subconscious and conscious brain, and you'll start having confidence in the idea. You'll also be "telling the universe," in a way. You're stating your absolute intent and expectation and it is being received.

Writing something down—a story, a hex, a prayer—helps make it real. My daughter rewrites her notes from class in different colors with little drawings, and she's got an A average (and is clearly a genius). Putting your thoughts into words gives them shape, structure, and import. Knot magic has the same impetus. Every knot that you make puts your intention into the work. It becomes an extension of your will out into the universe.

As such, introducing an element of ritual into your life is a wonderful way to enhance your mental health and your magical prowess. Consider muscle memory. This is the practice of repeating the same motion over and over—a tennis swing, a jump shot—until your body naturally knows what to do. This is a boon in physical and mental acuity. It also helps immensely with your magical practice.

Each of these steps makes your spell stronger. Each of them will get you in the correct frame of mind—calm, collected, focused. One of these is the statement "You are your deeds." This is more than walking the walk. This is stating that integrity is required. If you say it, you will do it. I've also found "You are your deeds" to be a way to try to eliminate sarcasm and gossiping from conversation.

The mundane action means that you have to *do* something. When I was stuck thinking that I couldn't have nice things, once Mark wiped the fog away from my eyes, I started applying for better jobs. Not just jobs, and not randomly applying for anything because I was so unhappy. I started applying for jobs that paid considerably more money that were closer to my home. I reached out to temp agencies and headhunters. I had friends read over my résumé. I applied with determination and the understanding that one of these jobs was mine.

It isn't enough to believe that you deserve something, you have to work on it too. To wish for something and then not do anything about it is a waste of time at best and whining at its worst.

As Ron Swanson in the television show *Parks and Recreation* says, "Never half ass two things. Whole ass one thing."[9] If you're going to be pouring belief, words, and action into something, don't waste your time. This is your life we're talking about.

ETHICS

I am not your mother, and I am not Oprah. I cannot be a beacon of ethical magic for you, because your moral compass lies within you. I can tell you the magics that I avoid. Not because I think

---

9. Michael Schur, dir., *Parks and Recreation,* season 4, episode 16, "Sweet Sixteen," aired February 23, 2012, on NBC, https://www.hulu.com/series /parks-and-recreation-93dc18da-96d9-4841-b125-40f901f7e7eb, min. 20.

that they're "bad magic" or because I don't think you should or shouldn't do magic at or on other people or other people's circumstances. I don't practice these because I think it's bad form. Just as tarot readings are not the answer to all of life's questions, magic is not the proper tool for all of life's problems. Your words have meanings. Again, the word *spells* is not a coincidence.

Also, these ethics are personal guidelines. I have magical friends who don't have a moment's worry about casting revenge or making promises that might not be possible to keep. That's okay too, but they can write their own books about their magical practices.

- You don't have to tear down other people's faith to make space for your own belief. You don't have to make smack talk a part of your practice. Let other people believe what they want.

- Do not make promises you don't intend to keep. Not to yourself, not to the universe, not to anyone else. This kind of dishonesty tends to boomerang at you.

- Use caution with revenge. I'm not going to waste time going on about the rule of three or "harm none, do as you will," which you won't care about unless you're Wiccan. These are irrelevant unless they're a part of your faith tradition. What I will tell you is that I have never seen or heard of someone casting a revenge or harmful spell on someone else without getting nicked by it too. The only revenge spell I do is a wish spell that the person is treated just the same as everyone is treated by them. Think of it as the magical equivalent of "I'm rubber and you're glue, whatever you say bounces off me and sticks to you."

- Using other people's hair or clothing can be manipulative outside of a protection spell. It goes against free will and can bind you to those people in unforeseen ways. You'll also become connected if you did a banishing on a person while using a part of them. That part is still with you, near you, and tangled in your magic. It's counterintuitive.

- Speaking of other people, ask permission before you use magic on other people. Even if you're just trying to help.

- Again, your words *matter*. What you say, who you say it to, the emotion that pushes your words out of your mouth—all of this matters. Be mindful.

Starhawk, a writer, activist, witch, feminist, and all-around badass, addresses power in her book *Truth or Dare*. She writes that there are three distinct types: power-over, power-with, and power-from-within.[10]

Power-over can be achieved with manipulation or force. It is represented in our time by the patriarchy and societal and institutional racism. The people who have been in power will use their power-over to keep the structures that put them in charge intact. We see this in the diminishing of people of color, queer folks, poor people, people with disabilities, and anyone else who lives on the margins. In interpersonal terms, power-over relates to gaslighting, emotional and physical abuse, and manipulation. Power isn't shared and doesn't change hands, especially to anyone who could be described as "other." The people in charge control the resources and, as a result, control others.

---

10. Starhawk, *Truth or Dare: Encounters with Power, Authority, and Mystery* (New York: HarperCollins, 1987), 9.

A good question is, is power-over always bad? Except in the case of a parent over a minor child or guardian over someone who is incapable of making clear decisions for themselves, I think it is. If my kids are still minors and engage in damaging behavior, it's my responsibility to protect them. Regardless of the means. If my sister has a diminished capacity and I want to help her, I will use all the tools available, including magic. Is this right? Ethical? I think so, but you might not. I can use a binding or a banishing charm on them without their permission, and my moral compass will be okay.

If I use magic on someone else, someone who is not part of my heart or blood family, that crosses a line for me. This is something you have to figure out on your own. There is a spell in here that sends negative energy back to the person who created it. It's a bit in the gray area for me, and I make sure that I don't send anything that didn't originate from the sender, but you might not be comfortable with that. You have to use your own compass to align your magic, but I will caution you that things tend to boomerang magically. The Wiccan belief that anything you do comes back to you threefold might be a consideration for you.

Power-with is communal power. You see this in balanced relationships and intersectional communities. This is shared power that can make change collectively. On a personal level, power-with is a healthy, loving relationship. It includes a work relationship that is fair and relationships between any other group of people who are nonexploitative. This is powerful magic when holding space for folks who are in marginalized communities. If you hold privilege, use it to give others space and power to be heard.

Power-from-within is about your inner strength. This is the kind of power that magic brings out of you. This should be the source of your spells and confidence. Power-from-within will guide you to the right folks to work with, to create power-with, and will help you plan your goals and dreams. This is the power that you use in your magic, whether alone or with community.

I bring this up because I think it's an important part of using your magic with integrity. I can't tell you how to treat people. I can tell you that power-over corrupts. Maybe not right away, but it always happens. If you want to have a long, healthy magical life, you would do well to practice the healthy powers and try to avoid the unhealthy.

One of the things that makes power-over so attractive is that it is the only one that does not make you vulnerable in some way. Vulnerability can be terrifying if you've spent your entire life avoiding it. It is an understandable behavior, but avoiding looking into yourself and finding all your sensitive spots can lead to being a type of reserved and distant that in turn can lead you right to power-over behavior.

Everyone has their own moral compass, and everyone will use their magic as they see fit. I can't lay a "you should, you shouldn't" chapter on ethics on you, but I can suggest that once you recognize your power, you must then decide how to use it. Do you want to be someone who is confident and easy to work with or someone who works magic for influence and fear-based respect? Just something to keep in mind.

TOOLS

I chose the magical tools in this book because these are what I have the most experience and luck with. I use them nearly every day, and I find that the more I use them, the better they work. Common tools that you can access are herbs and other plants; scrying objects such as crystal balls, bowls of water, and scrying

mirrors; and the ritual tools of Wicca and other practices, including an athame, pentacle, cup, bell, wand, or cauldron.

Some of the coolest tools I've ever seen were in the home of a
long-time tarot reader. I saw the scrying bowl made of a human
skull that was given to him from a holy man in Tibet. I saw the
deck of tarot cards he'd been reading for over sixty years, held together with cellophane tape and yellowed and faded so that only
he could tell which card was which. I saw bones for throwing.
A chair used by the members of the Golden Dawn. Books that
were well over 100 years old. The only thing that he used reg-
ularly was the deck of cards. The rest just sat there, unused and
unnecessary, except for the amazing historical interest. If you
don't use the tools, ask yourself if you need them.

I've seen beautiful singing bowls and magical knives that
were so old and worn they were needle thin. I've seen Wonder
Woman Pop! figures honored on altars. I've held wooden rosary
beads that vibrated with energy in my hands. I've seen a clear
quartz crystal that I gave to my dad for protection while he
worked as a police officer turn gray, then black, and then crack
and fall into pieces.

I have felt the energy of a house change when the owner
swept the floor, cleaned it with Florida water, and tossed the dirt
outside. It lifted and became cleaner and warmer. I have seen
faces change in the glow of a candle's light and after reading a
card.

These tools can be important and can make a difference.
They shouldn't make you worry about money, though. That's not
the point of them.

If you can't afford the tools, please don't hesitate to make your
own. It is so important to remember that the first magic wand

was a pointed finger. Do not allow your financial situation or lack of accessibility keep you from moving forward in your magical work.

The tools are not magical. They are not special. Just as tarot cards are just pieces of paper, magical tools are just tools. The magic is in the person holding the tool.

Chapter 4 explains more about magical supplies and tools and will give you a broader idea of what you can use.

RESULTS

How do you know when your magic has worked? How do you measure your time and energy and hold it up against the results? The best and easiest answer is journaling. You can start at the beginning of the entire process with a summary of what in your life you'd like to change. Document what you did in the spell crafting, and then check in every few weeks or so to track the change that you made. In Wiccan traditions, this journal is called a Book of Shadows. It tracks the growth that you've made in your magical life and can help you figure out what does and what does not work for you. I don't use herbs and am not a kitchen witch at all, but crystals and candles are totally my jam. I found this out by trying some spells with lavender and realizing that I really, really hate lavender. I also kill houseplants.

Another way to judge your results is to ask your close friends how your life has changed over a period of time. Our close friends have a perspective that we just can't access. It's hard to see the maze when you're in it. Think of it as asking someone if they can tell you've been lifting weights. Do your arms look better? Do they see a change in whatever you're magic-ing about?

TAKESIES BACKSIES

Sometimes you throw down a spell and then find out something new. Maybe the person you were furious with is not the person who caused the problem. Maybe the job you were so focused on has been overshadowed by a brand-new opportunity. So you have that magic hanging out there, but your intention has changed.

What I find works the best is to undo the magic. If you've written the spell, burn it. If you've tied knots, untie them. You've got the power to pull down what you've built. The important part of this is using the same amount of intensity that you did when you created the spell. I always throw in an apology to the universe and try to be more mindful in the future. It doesn't always work, but I try.

INTUITION

Intuition is that pull inside you that tells you what's going to happen next. It's like a radio trying to find a station. You hear, sense, and feel the energy around you. You always have, but the part that needs to be taught is the interpretation of it.

This is the thing that tells you who is about to call you before your phone rings. These are the dreams that show you a flash of what is in your future and the feelings you get when you meet someone who has ill intent for you. This is the source of the hairs on the back of your neck standing up. This is spidey-sense. In his book *Blink*, Malcolm Gladwell called it rapid cognition.[11] Precognition is divination through the psychic ability to see the future, including dreams that come true. A premonition is a warn-

---

11. Malcolm Gladwell, *Blink* (New York: Little, Brown, 2005).

ing about a future event. Intuition is your body's way of getting these messages to you.

It isn't just in your mind, so integrating your body and your awareness into your practice of intuition is important. When you feel a pull or a sensation in your body, check in. Sometimes when I am getting a "hit" of intuition, I can tell immediately where it's coming from. Other times it's completely random, and I can't see the connection anywhere.

Reading a person is also a skill that you can work into your intuitive practices. I am a very good judge of character. The times I've ignored my initial feelings about people have always gotten complicated. I observe people's body language and their faces. I see if the expressions on their faces match what I see in their eyes. Part of this is practice, and part is habit.

When working magic and deciding where to point your wand, check in with your intuition first. Everyone has intuition. Everyone. Some folks are just more tuned in to theirs than others. I've been working with tarot cards for over thirty years, so I've been exercising my intuition nearly every day. It's very much like a muscle, and the more you use it, the stronger it gets.

There are a few basic things that you can do to enhance your intuition:

- Trust yourself. We are often told that we're wrong, that we're overreacting, unstable, or whatever other form of gaslighting that's been flung at us. As often as you can, first consult with yourself and *then* with other people if you need to.

- Test yourself. Note your first impressions, hunches, and inspirations. Maybe you are thinking of a song and hear it on the radio later. If you're keeping a journal, you can make a list of when this happens. The more you notice your intuition, the stronger it gets.

- Challenge yourself. Write down what you think will happen in a certain situation. It doesn't have to be in your life—just something with an outcome you're sure to see. Who will win a Tony? Who will win the sports game? Will someone win the lottery? Write down your predictions and then what happened. Write how you picked up the information. Did you hear it? Did you see something? Train yourself to observe how your intuition works.

- Be discerning. Sometimes a dream is just your brain throwing bits of crazy at a wall to see what sticks. If you pull the Three of Swords for the day, I think it's okay to be alert that day but not to lock yourself in the house. If you feel you're having an intuitive flash about something, check the real world first. Is it possible? Is it likely?

- Get a buddy. I tell my husband *everything*. He's my best friend, so I can't help it. I told him that I was at a concert and thought about someone falling in the aisle and then a few seconds later, someone fell right next to me. When you talk about these things, it not only reinforces your intuition within yourself, but it also helps you verify your gift with friends.

- Listen to your body. If you're sick or tired, you won't be as able to clearly interpret your intuition.

- Pay attention to the room that you're in. Is it a place with high emotions? A funeral home, hospital, dorm? Is it filled with cranky people? How about toddlers? Any place that has a high emotion content is going to make you more vulnerable to an empathic overload. When you find yourself in

situations like this, ground, center, and shield. You'll learn
how to do this in chapter 3.

- Learn how to check in with yourself and the different parts
of your intuition. What this means is that you hold up the
hit you get, examine it, and then decide what to do with it.

I was once out to lunch with a friend and kept getting this
overwhelming feeling of dread. I couldn't figure out what was
wrong, but I was nearly in tears. I asked my friend if they were
okay. Yes. I looked around and everyone looked okay. After we
left, I pulled out on the highway to see a terrible car accident
that happened right near where we'd been eating. I don't know
if those two things are connected. That's one of the fun things
about intuition—sometimes you don't know. All I know for certain is that the feeling stopped as soon as I acknowledged the accident. I have had this happen with clients who are having med-
ical issues. When I ask, "Does your heart hurt? My heart hurts,"
my pain goes away as soon as they say yes.

BEWARE OF MAGICAL THINKING

There is such a thing as losing yourself in magical thinking. Not
every bad thing that happens is an omen. Not every sign is A
SIGN. Sometimes, shit just happens. It is possible to paralyze
yourself with anxiety, depression, or just a bad day, masquerad-
ing as an intuitive flash.

You can become so deeply entrenched in finding the meaning of life in your tea leaves or tarot cards and forget the point
of your life—to live it. It's easy to get distracted by the portents
and signs and forget to pay the phone bill. Magic is a tool and
needs to be used alongside the other tools that you have in this

life: your intellect, your sense of self, your common sense. These things are key resources and are more trustworthy than your intuition if you're upset, angry, or afraid.

If you find yourself faced with a dilemma, don't turn to magic first. Turn to your common sense. Ask a friend for advice and seek a different perspective. It's okay to question your intuition. Question it by getting another opinion, even if that opinion is your pendulum or tarot cards. Take your intuition seriously, but recognize that it's not the answer to all your problems.

The next section talks about finding your quiet space. This is a helpful practice for life's problems as well as preparing for spells. Calming yourself, clearing your mind, and analyzing the problems ahead of you can help you figure out your mundane problems as well. No magic required.

You are putting together your magical tool kit now. What can you pull from yourself and from the space around you? You are gearing up, very literally, to take your life into your hands. Be sure your tools are sharp, clean, and meaningful. Be sure that they're in your hands for a purpose. Be sure.

CHAPTER 3

Quiet Space and Ritual

When you walk into a temple or a church, there is a space at the front of the building that you just *know* is holy to those who worship there. Even if it's not your faith, you instinctively know that that's where belief lives. It's a focal point for hope, belief, fear, rage—all these feelings pointed in one direction. Repetition of prayers pointing to the same place. Chanting, singing, intent, and belief—everything aimed at one place, for decades.

That concentration of the mundane and the magical has an effect on places. The energy is shifted and shifted again. Emotions can make a place holy.

I started my own altar by accident. I had a candle holder with a little fox on it and some pretty stones and shells. Soon they were joined by a statue of the Black Madonna. It grew organically, and as I started becoming more comfortable with being a witch, it became a more important part of my life. My kids started adding things to it, and the care and keeping of the space became important to all of us.

Having a sacred space for your magical work isn't a necessity. I have friends who worship outside and leave no trace behind them after their spells are completed. What it can give you, though, is a home base and a space where your energy can be restored. Why do people go to church? To feel better, to feel at home, to feel comfort in ritual and the familiar rhythms of sights, smells, and sounds they've always known. This is the space that we're going to create.

There is a saying that I've seen around lately, that one person will "hold space" for another's grief or pain. This is a version of that. Your altar is holding space for you to be calm and to create magic.

One of the instructions you'll find in the spells is "go to your quiet place." There are a few reasons for this. First, you need to concentrate. Second, the more you use a space for magic, the more consecrated it becomes. Energy tends to collect where it's welcome and comfortable. With this in mind, find a place in your home where you can sit comfortably, with few distractions. I like working magic at my desk. I make sure my phone is silenced, my computer is turned off, and my animals are settled. I usually wait until my family has gone out or to sleep. I have a comfortable chair, candles, oils, and other tools stashed nearby, and I have enough space to do the tangible magic regardless of what it is. I work the magic at my desk and set the candle, stones, or any other tools that I've used on my altar when I'm finished.

This is my physical quiet place. To find my mental peace, I start by making sure I have all the tools that I'm going to use at hand and setting them out in front of me like a chef's *mise en place*.

I use my meditation app for at least ten minutes before I begin a spell. While I meditate, I don't think about the magic I plan to do but about calming my mind. I focus on my breathing and nothing else, and when it ends, I am wholly present in my magic.

Find a place in your house that works for you. If you're not at home, you'll need to cultivate a calm place wherever you are. There are ideas below for travel and hidden altars.

There are places in the world that feel as if magic has always lived there. In the mountains of New Mexico, some rumored to have cores of pure quartz, you can feel the vibration of the earth. On Venice Beach, if you sit still long enough, your heart will match the ocean's waves. I have heard that when you stand at Newgrange in Ireland, you lose all touch with time. It is as if all the years of belief have stored up and are waiting for you to tap into them.

PRAYER

Prayer helps you create your intention. Intent is a huge part of magic. The only difference that I see between prayer and intent is that prayer seems to have a hand out to someone, asking them to join you in your magic: dear god, goddess, lady, universe, ancestor, please intercede for me if you can and help me get through this ordeal or to this goal.

I don't think that you need to belong to any faith tradition to pray. I have a strong connection with Mary and I'm not Christian. Her icons and symbols have always shown up for me in my life, and I truly believe that God shows up for folks in ways that they can understand. If you feel like someone out there is looking out for you, good for you. I don't care if it's Jesus or Wonder Woman or Freya. If there is someone you can relate to, figure out why and what qualities appeal to you. Usually those things are indications of traits that you've found in people you admire or something you're striving for personally.

The world is too lonely and disconnected for you to feel shame or reticence about embracing someone who gives you comfort. However, I encourage you to be respectful and learn about the history and culture that your prayer target comes from.

Some folks did not grow up in a religious household and may not know how to pray. It's very similar to getting to your quiet place. This is the way I pray most effectively, and ritualizing your prayer can help you stay consistent in the practice:

- Close your eyes. It decreases distraction.
- Either out loud or in your head, address the entity you're praying to. This gives the prayer a clear beginning.
- Start a conversation. You don't have to be formal if you don't want to be. The relationship that you have with this entity is all yours.
- Control the conversation. The content of prayer is up to you. There does not need to be an exchange if you're asking for something. This isn't bargaining. You can ask to be looked over. To be given strength. To see clearly. You can also just say hi.
- Say something in closing: Thank you. I love you.

Here's an example that I used to say after I tucked my kids in at night: "Hey, universe. Please help them dream of beautiful things and keep them safe in your sight. Amen."

Simple, straightforward, easy to remember.

Another is one that I've carried around in my head since I was little: the first verse of "Be Not Afraid." It's a song, but I use it as a prayer.

The prayer doesn't have to be at or about or to anyone. Its job is to help you feel better.

Madeleine L'Engle used what she calls "St. Patrick's Rune" in her book *A Swiftly Tilting Planet* to help give her characters guidance and courage. Attributed to St. Patrick, the poem is an old Celtic prayer that resonates with me. It just *feels* holy.

> At Tarah to-day in this fateful hour,
> I place all Heaven with its power,
> And the sun with its brightness,
> And the snow with its whiteness,
> And fire with all the strength it hath,
> And lightning with its rapid wrath,
> And the winds with their swiftness along their path,
> And the sea with its deepness,
> And the rocks with their steepness,
> And the earth with its starkness,—
> > All these I place,
> > By God's almighty help and grace,
> Between myself and the powers of darkness.[12]

I wanted to talk about prayer in this book, even though it's meant to be magic without religion, because I want to encourage those who have lived separately from religion to feel comfortable picking up the phone and talking to whoever will answer on the other line. Be sure you're asking folks who are going to help

---

12. James Clarence Mangan, "St. Patrick's Hymn before Tarah," in *Library of the World's Best Literature,* vol. 17, ed. Charles Dudley Warner (New York: The International Society, 1897), lines 39–51, https://www.bartleby.com/library/poem/3415.html.

and not harm, but other than that, I think prayer makes us feel less alone.

RITUAL

A ritual is a ceremony with a series of actions completed in a specific order. This is all the weight that you need to bring to this word. A ritual *can* be lots of things. It can be found in every religion, every sports team, every daily task. Brushing your teeth is a ritual. You've done it the same way since you were a kid. Wet toothbrush, apply toothpaste, brush, rinse, put toothbrush down.

This makes brushing your teeth a mindless task. This is a good thing, as you're less likely to make mistakes. You have gained the muscle memory to brush your teeth flawlessly. You can teach someone to do it with little effort, and you can slide into a quiet meditation while you're in the middle of it. You also have the confidence that you're doing it right.

These are all the same reasons that ritual is important in magic. Of course you can do magic off the cuff—it's like breathing—however, if you're intent on making a change in your life, you need to have familiarity with your tools; a beginning, a middle, and an end; and the confidence in your movements that comes from practice.

Magic is just like any other skill. You have to practice and study to be good at it. The more time you put into it, the better you get at it. There is a theory that you become a master of a task after having performed it for 10,000 hours. I know this to be true in my life. In tarot, as a parent, as a partner, I had to put in time and energy to learn how to be good at it. Magic is no different. A daily or monthly practice is just the thing to get you where you need to be.

Here is my recommended format for creating a ritual. It's both easy and complicated. This works for big magic or small magic, and you can adjust the ritual to suit you.

1. Turn off all distractions.
2. Physically clean your working area.
3. Use incense or other herbs to clear the energy of the space.
4. Arrange your tools.
5. Draw a circle around you.
6. Ground and center, meditate, or both.
7. Begin the spell.
8. End the spell.
9. Break the circle.
10. Clear the tools.
11. Dissipate the energy you've gathered.

You're going to need a space that you can assure is as distraction free as possible. You can also write this list down (I always forget the last part) until it's in your head firmly. You can practice the spell before you do it. Make sure you have all your tools. Get your head together, get your breath under control, and give the process the respect it deserves.

Even with distractions, your intent is the most important thing in a ritual. My kids used to put their pajamas on inside-out and flush ice cubes down the toilet in hopes of a snow day the next day. This ritual is just as important as any you'd find in a church. When it worked and school was canceled the next day, I would hear, "We did it! It worked!" Absolute validation that their spell did its job. When it didn't work, they would put their heads together to come up with additional steps to add to the ritual so that next time they would totally get a snow day.

It's the same thing with us. When we ritualize anything in our day, we bring a calmness and sacredness to it. Just like shuffling the cards before a tarot reading calms the reader and puts them in the right headspace, having a familiar pattern of activity before spell work will put you there as well.

Another important part of ritual is to remove damaging emotions from your work. I am a big fan of anger. It burns away apathy and is a fierce motivator. It will also mess with your focus and flood your brain with *feelings*. Ugh. Feelings are so, so important, but there is a time and a place for them. Creating and manifesting your entire destiny is not the right time to use your anger. Following an established ritual (practice, practice) will help push the emotions to the side so that you can truly focus on your work.

Szeptem is a Polish word that means "in a whisper," which is a way of sending a spell on the winds. It's used to enchant objects. I learned this word after watching my Polish grandparents whisper prayers under their breath. I watched this for years and years. Sometimes it was an under-the-breath swear. I found out a few years ago that they likely learned that from their parents, who learned it from their parents, and so on. Rituals like this that last for generations have lasted this long for a reason. They work.

You can chant, meditate, or ritualize all the inner distractions away from your work and try to minimize the effect of the outer distractions. When you do this, you'll find that your body is calm, your breath is steady, and your focus is absolute.

Casting a Circle

Let's talk about the space in which you work. Casting a circle is an important part of Wiccan practice (I keep talking about Wicca because it is a well-known magical practice). What it does is contain the energy you're working with. It keeps some things out and other things in and creates a sacred space. Circles can be made with the light of a candle, formed with a line of salt, drawn with incense, lined with candles, drawn with a grubby little finger, or imagined.

I clean off my altar entirely, taking off all the stones and tchotchkes and statuary. I wipe it down and light a single candle in the middle. At the end of the spell, I light a candle to close it out and let those burn until they're finished. My circle is drawn with fire in my mind. I have friends who traditionally "call the corners or quarters" and place candles in all four points of the compass. I know folks who visualize a bubble surrounding them entirely and they work in that. It is helpful to have a clear beginning and a clear end to your spell crafting, so I encourage you to try out a few different things to mark out your workspace to see what works for you.

INTENTION

I think that the use of prayer is a small ritual that you can engage in to center your mind and calm your soul. You can use prayer *with* ritual to enhance it. You can ritualize the prayer so that you create a mantra to carry you through the ritual. Try everything. See what works for you.

Prayer + Ritual = Intention

The clearer you set your intention, the stronger your magic will be. For example, your intention might be "I want to be rich."

Well, fantastic. Some ways that that can happen are a divorce settlement, an inheritance from a deceased parent, or a settlement from a car accident.

Let's be more specific.

You need money, and you want it to come from someplace that doesn't cause harm. You want to focus on what the money will *do* for you, not just having it, so you set your intention like this: "I will always have my needs met. I am grateful, I welcome the money that will find me, and with it I will _____. I will be happy to receive blessings from the universe, if it harms none."

This kind of accuracy in words and thoughts comes up countless times in fairy tales and stories. You meet a magical creature and wish for gold, and then everything you touch turns to gold. You want to sleep and wake 100 years later. You ask for help and promise your future to the helper, and in exchange, they take your child. Fairy tales—the originals—are cautionary tales about trusting the otherworld and how fairies can kick your ass up between your shoulder blades if you speak to them with the wrong words.

You can encourage the money to find you with some spells that you'll find later in the book, but your intention is incredibly important. Be clear. Be consistent.

Also, remember your ethics. Belief creates words, which create action. All these steps lean on the next to make things happen. You have to have follow through with magic. Anointing and lighting a prosperity candle and then going on a shopping spree is not effective magic. It's a waste of a good candle—and of your time.

YOUR ALTAR

An altar is any flat-topped area that serves as a focus for your magical work. You can purchase an altar or build one on a shelf. Mine has been on an old telephone table, a bookshelf, and, now, on top of a bookcase. I keep mine fresh by following the moon cycles. This is an ideal thing to have in your house if you're doing candle magic, knot magic, or working with stones or crystal grids. Mine is delightfully out of the way of the cats and is undisturbed. I also keep statuary that is important to me on it. Sometimes it's the Black Madonna, and sometimes it's my Wonder Woman statue. It depends on the energy I want to pull into my magical work. This month, it's a Pop! figure of Freddie Mercury.

Think of your altar as your magical office. You need to keep it tidy, keep it focused on the work that you're doing, and keep it undisturbed. You might even have to keep it hidden if your folks or partner aren't very cool with the magic thing.

You can consecrate your altar with oil or smoke from incense or candles. You can bless it and imagine the energy that you're building as the heartbeat of your home. Imagine its light shining and filling your house with a steady pulse of love, protection, and energy. Allow your family to add to your altar if they understand that it's a sacred space to you.

My altar has gone through several iterations. It's moved several times as we've shifted furniture around and acquired more cats. What once was a collection of pretties is gradually becoming the heartbeat of our home. You can't mistake it for anything other than a sacred place.

Every month on the new moon, clean your altar. Wipe it down and get all the incense ashes cleaned up. Remove all the rocks that were hanging out and charging with good energy all month. Take off all the statues and wipe them down. Thank them for being your guardians for the month. Use an all-natural cleanser to scrub the top of the altar until it shines, and then light a white candle and place it in the middle of the altar. Use a cleansing herb (sage, cedar, or lavender) to clear the energy around the altar, the air above and in front of it, and below if you can. Let it sit empty except for the candle for a day.

That night, write down your goals for the month. This doesn't have to be *Middlemarch*. Write a few that will help you focus on your overall goals.

Goals for July

- Go to the gym at least five times a week.
- Clean out that one cabinet that keeps trying to kill me with flying Tupperware.
- Meditate every morning for at least five minutes.

Take that paper and find a stone or a statue that matches how you feel. Are you feeling anxious? How about some jet? Are you needing some comfort? You might reach for your statue of Lady of Guadalupe or Kwan Yin statue or Pearl from *Steven Universe* figurine. Fold your paper three times and place it under this figure. That plants the intention for your month.

Throughout the month, you're going to add things to the altar as you complete your magic: candles, incense, tokens, and knotted cords. There is a spell in chapter 8 for a small money altar to leave on your big altar. As you collect these things, your space is going to get cluttered and messy. Good. Leave it that way. Life is messy and your workspace should reflect that accurately. Just be careful with your candles and incense, and you should be good.

At the next new moon, start it all over again.

Travel Altar

Sometimes you've got to go to Los Angeles for eight days and do readings every day and read at parties at night. You're leaving behind not only your altar but also your family and pets and security. You have to be "on" and do approximately twenty readings in seven days, plus travel, which makes you incredibly whiny. What's the solution? Travel altar.

Find a small box, such as a cigar box, and toss all the things in it that you might need—a small tea light candle, matches, a cone of incense. You can clear the energy of your hotel room and then set up a little altar. When I'm in new towns, I always buy stones and put them up around my tiny altar while I'm there. It gives me a place that feels like home, where I can be calm and still. TSA thinks it's weird, so heads up when you go through airport security.

Secret Altar

It is hard to come out of the broom closet. Magic makes people nervous, and the trappings of magic make them even more anxious. People who are nervous or afraid can often lash out in damaging ways.

If you're sharing space with someone who is afraid of magic, the safest thing to do is to create your altar in a hidden space. If you think that that makes you less of a witch, just remember that the universe sees you and understands what you're going through. It's really okay.

I have friends and clients who have created altars under their beds, in closets, and at friends' houses. I often recommend that people use boxes to store their altars. If you have a shoebox or cigar box, you can fill it with the gear that you need for your monthly spells. I'd recommend tea lights for your candle work. You can use a colored Sharpie to bring that energy into the spell and write on the bottom of the candle. Carry your box in your backpack or purse to a safe space to do your work. Don't worry if you have to blow out your candle instead of letting it burn out. Be sure it's 100 percent out before you put it back in the box.

The traveling altar can also be used secretly. Find a mint tin and keep a small candle, matches, and chalk in it. Keep a few small stones in there too. Open it up when you have work to do, do the work, and snap it closed when you're finished. Instant altar.

You can also keep a digital altar. I know this sounds odd, but work with me here. Keep a document on your computer or a note on your phone. You can add pictures to it. Use it as a small journal. You can create your magical space throughout the month, and at the next new moon, you can delete it. Magic travels, you know. Just be safe.

GROUNDING AND CENTERING

For years, I heard the words *grounding and centering* over and over and over. They seemed super important, but I honestly had no idea what they really meant. It was suggested to ground and center before doing magic or a tarot reading or going into a stressful meeting.

I've learned through trial and error and reading a lot of books that what this boils down to is remaining in the skin you're in during times when you need to concentrate. It's very easy to get carried away by worry or being preoccupied, and if part of you is gone, it makes whatever you're about to embark on more difficult than it needs to be.

The end goal of grounding and centering is to make yourself calm and collected. I always imagine emotion to be like water and the brain as an electrical circuit board. If your emotion floods out your brain, you're going to make bad decisions and your attention will be scattered. The point of magic is to take control of your life, and it's important to have both hands on the wheel when you work your spells.

Even if you're in an airplane or in a car, you can do this exercise. You know where the ground is. Your job is to send your energy down as far as you need until you hit the earth. Allow yourself to push your energy out until you feel anchored to the planet. Then, you can relax and know that you are secure.

Grounding is the calm part of "calm and collected." It's going to get you into a place where any upset you might be feeling or impulses that come to you can easily be turned away until you're finished with your work.

The best meditation I've learned for grounding is tied to its connection to your root chakra. It's easy to remember, because all you're doing is imagining a tree growing right out of you.

How to ground: Sit or stand still. Imagine a seed growing into a tree in your body. I usually imagine it's growing in the center of me, starting at my lower back. Watch the seed grow into a sapling, and feel the roots grow down your legs and into the earth. Watch the top of the tree branch out, and feel the branches grow through your head, shoulders, and arms. Visualize the branches growing down in a graceful arc to touch the ground. Visualize the roots growing down and back up in an arc to touch the surface of the earth. Now you're encircled by the earth. You are well and truly rooted to the ground and will feel steady and ready for your work.

Here are some ways to perform a quick grounding:

- Toss some rocks in your pockets or your bra.
- Eat something.
- Have (safe, consensual, awesome) sex.
- Pet an animal.
- Sit down on the earth.
- Literally hug a tree.
- Smell some flowers.
- Hug someone.

Centering is the act of becoming mindful. You're not in the past with sadness or regret, and you're not in the future with anxiety and worries. You're right here and now. All of your selves and your thoughts are collected into one place and time. This is also called being mindful. Mindfulness is a state of being in which you are wholly present and wholly focused on what you're doing. It can be achieved by meditation, and with practice, you can achieve mindfulness in just a few minutes.

Centering is important in magic because if your mind is split, your attention is split and you are not putting your whole self into what you intend to do. Having a fully aligned body, mind, and soul makes for better magic. Remember: thoughts, words, deeds. Getting your mind right will make your magic tighter and more effective.

The exception to this is passion- or anger-fueled magic that welcomes your chaos. There is a spell later on in the book that is fueled by rage. This is the only time I've felt it was unnecessary to be grounded before doing a spell. Anger turns into resentment or pity if it's tucked away too long. Best to let it out, constructively, while it's fresh.

There are a lot of ways to learn how to center, but the end goal is always the same: you want to be in your quiet place. This is going to look a little different to everyone, so I'll make it as generic as I can.

The quiet place is you, with a calm mind, clear intent, and steady hand. You are not distracted, not living in the past or the future. You are focused and not giving attention to every thought that is going through your mind. You are *present*. This is the starting point. This is your quiet place.

These are a few different ways to get to your quiet place. Try them all out until you find one that works for you.

Focus on an object. If you are using a candle, for example, in a spell, pay attention to it with all your senses. What does it smell like? How does it feel in your hands? What is the weight of it? How many colors are swirling together in the wax? While you're observing, regulate your breathing. When a stray thought comes, just let it leave the way it came in.

Dr. James Doty suggests an excellent mindfulness technique in his meditations, which are taught in his book *Into the Magic Shop*.[13] It is adapted here:

- Find your quiet space (see page 48). Be sure you won't be interrupted.

- Be sure that you're calm in mind, body, and spirit.

- Decide your intention for this exercise: What do you want?

13. James Doty, *Into the Magic Shop: A Neurosurgeon's True Story of the Life-Changing Magic of Compassion and Mindfulness* (London: Yellow Kite, 2016), 79.

- Imagine that you are outside your body looking at yourself.
- Start at your toes and relax each one. Do this with your feet, your legs, and all the way up to the top of your head.
- If you get distracted, back to the toes with you. Just think about each group of muscles relaxing. Remember to breathe.
- Feel yourself becoming more grounded, more centered in your quiet space.
- As you work your way up your body, picture what you want happening. Imagine what it will feel, taste, and smell like. See yourself in the place of receiving.
- Stay in that place as long as you're able.
- You're going to feel a little floaty—you might even fall asleep. This is okay. Go with it.

Hold that feeling close to you for the rest of your day.

When you're in this space, magic comes easily. Intention setting comes easily. You can reach this place fairly quickly with practice, and you can set intentions that work. You can also create this safe space while you're out in the world. Try to create a field of calm around you. You don't have to go full Glinda the Good Witch, but it's good if you can visualize the boundaries. I imagine my aura—the energy surrounding all living things— having an adamantium or vibranium shield around me. (Hi, I'm a nerd.) I do this when I'm somewhere I feel uncomfortable. I'm a fairly anxious person, so I do it a lot. Before I go into a store, I sit in my car and create my bubble. I put my aura suit on and head into the fray. I have my earbuds in and my partner or kids with me and focus on getting what I need and getting out. When

I get back to the car, I let it fall off. Sometimes, I can actually feel it falling away from me. Makes me really happy that I had it in the first place.

I also put little blessings on my kids and loved ones by tracing hearts or protective sigils on them when I give them hugs. I use the quiet space energy to transfer some of my love to them. In my head, it sparkles.

Grounding Tree

Have you ever felt like you had so much energy inside you that you were going to burst? Sometimes instead of channeling our energy and emotions properly, we let them build up. This can happen with your magical energy as well.

If you're feeling overwhelmed and like you're vibrating a little bit or your hands are hot and shaky, you can get a release with the help of a tree. Sit on your bottom, lean against the tree, and put your hands flat against the grass. Imagine all that excess energy going into the ground. Release the tension and anxiety that might have built up and send it all into the earth. She can take it.

BOUNDARIES

Sometimes you get overloaded with energy. It's just entirely too much. It's important to have boundaries—both internal and external boundaries—so that your empathic self doesn't get bombarded by other people's feelings. Empathic people pull in other people's energy and feelings, and they sometimes have a hard time telling which feeling is whose. It can be overwhelming, isolating, and scary. You go to a party, and instead of feeling happy or engaged, you find yourself in the corner of the house, overwhelmed by the amount of energy in the room. It hits you right in the face, and you can't get around or away from it. You start internalizing it and feel like everyone is looking at you or talking about you. You leave and then immediately think that you did something wrong.

One of the problems that come along with strong empathy is that we forget that even positive energy is energy. It's still over-stimulating and hard to take in. Your boundaries are what make it stop cold. Placing boundaries is super difficult if you weren't raised with them. You have to mess up a lot before you realize that you've reached adulthood with no real idea of where your space ends and another's begins.

I want to talk about external boundaries and why they're so important. In tarot readings, they're incredibly valuable in making it clear who you will read for, if you're going to get paid, and why. In life, they're important because you can't live your life for other people.

It just won't work.

Consider your life as a piece of Play-Doh. You start as this amorphous blob, and whatever needs or responsibilities are pushed upon you change your shape. Before long, your parents, society, culture, peers, television—you name it—have pushed and distorted you into a shape that maybe you weren't meant to be in. So when you're a teenager, or even maybe later, you start pushing and prodding *yourself* into a shape that makes sense to you, that feels good to you.

I want you to consider what you would do if you were building something wholly yours and someone came up and poked it. You'd lose your goddamn mind—and rightly too.

I want you to hold this idea in your head when someone asks you for a favor. Or when they send you a many-paged text bomb about how your behavior didn't match their expectations of you. Or when they make you feel small or stupid or wrong. I want you to imagine that they're poking you, regardless of the tools they use. If they're using guilt, or shame, or any other kind of emotional manipulation. I encourage you to lose your *mind*.

It is not your responsibility to behave in a way that conforms to other people's visions of who you are.

Learning boundaries is not generally taught to us; it's something we have to learn. As a middle-aged Midwestern woman, I have been establishing my boundaries my whole life, and the ones that I put up now stay there. It didn't happen that way to begin with, but I followed a few steps to make them permanent. It's not always easy, and sometimes you're going to lose friends or opportunities, but you'll be yourself and you'll be in the "you" shape that suits you best.

Am I being a dick or am I creating strong boundaries? A list:

- Do I want to do this? Do I want to do this favor, chore, or ask that is outside of my usual comfort zone?

- Does this person make me feel good? This is important. People who respect your boundaries will seldom make you feel small or ungrateful.

- Be sure that you have tiered friends. Protect yourself from folks who are not in for the long haul. Tier one: 3 a.m. phone call, I tell you everything, I trust you implicitly. Tier two: brunch, hanging out, surface problems. Tier three: surface only. This protects you from your (possibly Midwestern) inclinations to toss your heart at every person you meet to see if it sticks.

- Don't have floppy boundaries. It's confusing for you and your path, as well as the people around you. If you don't gossip with one friend, don't gossip with strangers, either.

Maintain your accessibility in a way that makes you happy and healthy.

- Remember that strong boundaries are part of self-care. You're not being selfish or rude—you're protecting yourself. Just as I don't read the news because it damages my happiness, I protect myself from negative people for the same reason. My happiness, my life. My boundaries are there to protect me and mine.

- When doing readings, exchange even practice ones for coffee or a meal. Don't undervalue your time, please. If you charge for readings, charge for the experience, not the minute. Your time is valuable.

- As seen on the internet: you don't have to set yourself on fire to keep other people warm.

What if the one who is poking you ... is you? What if you have internal boundaries that you keep floppy so that you can become comfortable with an okay life? Oh, that one stung. Goddamnit.

Just as external boundaries shape your life, internal boundaries make your life safer and happier. But they're hard! Crutches are used because we're limping, right? We can't use them forever or we won't ever walk straight.

The internal boundaries that need reinforcing are your self-esteem, your physical health, your mental health, and your emotional well-being. A lot of the time, your self-esteem is victim to the boundaries crashing all around. Sleep well, eat good food, and move your body. These three things power the meat sack that you wander about in, yes, but when you feel like garbage, you are less able to handle the things that life throws at you and start doubting yourself.

Saying no can help you shape your life externally. It works internally, too, but it's harder. In motivation, negativity just isn't as successful as positive reinforcement. If I try to quit smoking and talk shit about myself *to* myself, I'm more likely to smoke again. I have to be nice to myself to stay healthy.

I have a few tips to help you structure some healthy internal boundaries. These are just as important as your external boundaries. It'll help if you imagine yourself as a little kid, before all of the universe landed on you.

- Imagine that what you're doing to yourself, you're also doing to them, your inner child. Smoking? Not good for anyone, but especially not your inner child. They don't deserve that, and it's your job to protect them. Do your job.

- When you engage in negative self-talk, argue with it. Thoughts are just thoughts; feelings are just feelings. Identify the negativity, tell it to go away, and then state something that you're grateful for.

- Gratitude eats anxiety for breakfast. This is true. It's nearly impossible to have a dejected state of mind when you live in a place of gratitude.

- Breathing is the key to life. Breathe in for a count of four, hold it for a count of four, breathe out for a count of four, and so on. Your whole demeanor will change.

- If you need meds, go get meds. If you can't make your own serotonin reuptake inhibitors, store-bought is fine. The world is a hard enough place without placing additional hobbles on your legs. The story of suffering feeding your art is nonsense. Go get well.

- Help someone else. If you find that you're entirely in your head and can't seem to see your way clear, try to help someone else. Even just a little.

- Find space for a spiritual life. Even if it's just walking with children in nature. Even if it's meditating once a day. Even if it's volunteering with animals or going to a synagogue or mosque or church for an hour a week. Step outside your head and live in your soul for a bit.

- Have a routine. It's hard to beat yourself up for procrastination if you have a routine and stick to it. I know it's hard to do this sometimes, so start small with a bedtime and a regular wake-up time.

- Go see a therapist. Get out that weight you've been carrying around. I've gotten counseling for anxiety, depression, writer's block, and postpartum depression in my life. Every time, it helped—every time.

- Remember that your best will change depending on how you feel. Do your best, whatever that means at the time.

Please take it easy on yourself. It's a weird world out there, and we need to keep ourselves safe.

CHAPTER 4

Magical Tools and Supplies

Your magical supplies include anything that you use to enhance, perform, or engage with magic. This can be as mundane as a lighter or as complex as a blessed, oiled, engraved candle. Your tools are yours to choose and care for. I am a very casual practitioner of magic in the way that I approach it. There are no ceremonial robes in my house. My magic knife is a kitchen knife that I got from my grandma. The candles I use are purchased at the *mercado* in my city for about $2 each.

You *can* have some pretty cool tools. You can absolutely have these. You just don't *need* them. You don't need to drop $100 on a ritual athame if you can't swing it. It doesn't matter. The integrity of your magic will stay the same. Your altar can be a shelf in your kitchen or a room all its own.

I recommend finding some witches in the community who use tools and talk to them about what they use. Every person uses different things, and it's good to have conversations so you can see what will work best for you.

CORDS

Knot magic, also known as cord magic, can be used to bind an intention or to release it. Think of it as a little pouch. When you tie the knot, you bind the intention inside it. This is a quick, easy magical tool that you can use for almost anything—health, wealth, to hold your attention or focus, and so on. You can use anything from thread to rope to scarves to hair to create the knots and can put in charms or beads for a little symbolic push. You can use natural cord if you want to burn or bury it. I always keep something on hand too. You never know. Some folks who are far craftier than I are spinning their own cords. This is an amazing way to be 100 percent certain of what's in your tool and to invest as much energy in it as you want.

You tie the knot: the spell is cast. You untie or burn the knot: the spell is released. When I was in junior high, knotted friendship bracelets were huge. Someone would make bracelets out of a series of knots and give them to their friends. I wore one for about six years straight and never took it off. When it finally broke, I felt a small sense of loss. I can't really describe it. It was as if I had been given a little bit of grace, and when the bracelet broke, that grace dispersed.

Cords perform powerful magic and are used to bind the intent into the working. You are using your hands and skills to build something tangible, and there is magic in that action alone. Making and unmaking—these are the two sides of the universe. Each causes a shift in the energy of the universe, and having a hand in these shifts is powerful stuff. Even tying a knot makes a shift.

If you know any fierce knitters or crocheting folks, stay on their good side. These arts are a great way to put intent into a blanket or a scarf. With every knotted piece of yarn, plans can be made … and unmade.

STONES, CRYSTALS, AND ROCKS

Crystals and rocks shift your energetic vibration. We're moving forward on the assumption that magic is the place between what we know and what we don't. I'm a firm believer that if something makes you feel better and doesn't hurt you or anyone else, you should go for it. I love rocks and have been called a geomancer. They help me feel grounded, they cheer me up, and they are something substantive to hold on to when I'm anxious. I will generally have two rocks in my pockets and one or two in my bra at any given time. If it's a placebo effect, fine. I'm not mad about it.

A friend who knows me really well once gave me a hematite necklace. I was going through a hard time, and he put it around my neck, telling me I needed to be "here" more often. Present. Happy. Here. I started to feel better almost immediately. Maybe it was the energy of my friend who loved me. But I left and kind of forgot about the necklace. I started feeling calmer. I felt more capable of dealing with whatever flew my way. I kept the necklace on all the time and started noticing that I was changing. I felt more present—all the things that my friend wished for me. So I looked up the properties of hematite. It is a stone for protection that helps you stay grounded. It absorbs negative energy and helps you stay calm. It's connected to the root chakra, which is the one that's located at your tailbone.

I started calling it my "spiritual choke chain." When I wore it, I felt more grounded. That's it. That's the extent of its energy. *But,* when I felt more grounded, I also felt more capable and confident. That was *my* magic jumping in to fill the gaps.

Stones and crystals are amazing and beautiful magical tools for you to carry in your toolbox. They take the energy of their environment as well as the energy that the minerals inside them hold. You can find them at new age shops, rock and crystal fairs, or my favorite place, gift shops near national monuments. It's so odd, but every one that I've been to has crystal or rock bins, and they're crazy inexpensive. You can also find them online, which is helpful if you're looking for a specific stone. I will warn you that they're habit-forming, and you will likely find yourself in front of a table of stones asking, "Who wants to come home with me? All of you? Okay!" Best to bring a friend along. And have a safe word.

Stones and crystals are useful for filling in a missing element in yourself. When you're feeling afraid, you can carry some carnelian or blood stone. Feeling lighthearted and loving? Rose quartz. You can place them on your altar or near your workspace. You can also build crystal grids by placing stones and crystals in specific places to balance the energies in your home or in your life. One of the best side effects of collecting and using stones is that it's a great way to figure out when to come out of the broom closet. If you're not sure if that person at work will be nice when they find out you do magic, place a pretty rock on your desk and see if they comment on it. If they just say it's a pretty paperweight, you're probably dealing with a Muggle. If they grab it, say that it *feels* good, and ask what it "does," they're one of us.

After a while, you'll want to clean your stones. Some stones change under direct sunlight or dissolve in water, so be sure to do your research before you clean them. You can put them in running water; the sink is fine. Put them in the sunlight to soak up that warmth. You can also leave them outside on the full or dark moon to pull in the energy.

Properties

Here is a list of stones and their properties. You can use the properties to decide which rocks you need in your pocket today or which will work best in a spell.

Agate: Stability, grounding, confidence

Alexandrite: Health, calming, recovery

Amber: Balance, luck, positivity

Amethyst: Relaxation, sleep, insight

Apatite: Energy, clarity, inspiration

Aquamarine: Intuition, calming, clarity

Bloodstone: Energy, courage, happiness

Bone: Protection, energy, representation of animal

Calcite: Energy, purification, activation of energy

Carnelian: Confidence, energy, inspiration

Chalcedony: Calming, peace, happiness

Chrysocolla: Energy, willpower, confidence

Chrysoprase: Kindness, love, happiness

Citrine: Happiness, growth, confidence

Fluorite: Sleep, calming, positivity

Garnet: Energy, grounding, invigoration

Hematite: Grounding, grounding, like a spiritual thunder shirt

Jade: Luck, prosperity, wisdom

Jasper: Courage, mental acuity, strength

Jet: Grounding, positivity, luck

Kyanite: Meditation, balance, transformation

Labradorite: Intuition, magic, protection

Lapis Lazuli: Wisdom, awareness, enlightenment

Lepidolite: Calming, happiness, transformation

Malachite: Transformation, clarity, insight

Moldavite: Transformation, healing, is an intergalactic space pickle

Moonstone: Healing, inspiration, intuition

Muscovite: Intuition, agility, stimulation

Obsidian: Protection, calming, clarification

Onyx: Protection, strength, stamina

Opal: Healing, intuition, happiness

Pearl: Honesty, clarity, integrity

Peridot: Abundance, joy, confidence

Pyrite: Abundance, protection, clarity

Quartz: Clarity, healing, manifestation

Rhodochrosite: Treat yourself, confidence, joy

Rhodonite: Calming, insight, grounding

Rose Quartz: Love

Sardonyx: Protection, strength, happiness

Selenite: Cleansing, purification, positivity

Sodalite: Confidence, peace, relaxation

Sunstone: Creativity, energy, joy

Topaz: Healing, energy, honesty

Tourmaline: Protection

Turquoise: Honesty, open conversation, connection
to the universe

Unakite: Abundance, healing, love

Pockets of Rocks

The easiest thing to do with stones is to put them in your pockets or your bra if you wear one. At the beginning of your day, assess what you might need for the day. Having a comfort stone with you will give you the energy that you need as well as give you something that you can hold on to if you're feeling nervous. It's a comfort to have a familiar weight against your side if you're feeling challenged.

Here are a few stones paired with situations in which they could ground you:

Interview: Bloodstone

Free-Floating Anxiety: Chrysoprase

First Date: Rhodonite

Depression: Lepidolite

Stressful Family Situation: Tourmaline

Nightmares: Amethyst, blue chalcedony, lapis lazuli, jade, chrysoprase, smoky quartz

Imagine having a small person in your care. They have a bad dream, and you can place a magical stone in their little hand. So comforting. Using stones to help with your day-to-day problems has become so common that you can literally type "stones for nightmares" in a search engine and have a list to choose from.

I keep my stones in bowls around my house. If I have some anxiety or other concerns before I leave the house, I carefully select the stones that help me feel better. Sometimes if everything is okay, I'll just pick whichever stone I feel like carrying. Maybe because it's pretty or feels good in my hand. These can act as the original fidget spinner and be along for the ride purely to have a worry stone to hold on to.

Building a Crystal Grid

For a more intense and prolonged assist from stones, you can use a crystal grid. These can be set in any pattern that resonates with you and with the stones that can push forth your energy and intent.

Crystal grids are the deliberate placement of stones and crystals in such a way as to hold the energy of an intention. Think of it as a spiderweb of energy. Putting the crystals in the right place holds that intention, and the web that they create together acts as a battery for your spells. My son created a crystal grid under his bed when he was little without knowing what they were. I noticed some stones under his bed and asked if he dropped them. He said, "No, I just put them there to help me sleep, and they work."

Use a crystal grid when you're working on long-term plans that need a sustained source of energy. You can't maintain concentration for a month at a time, so the grid will hold the intention and focus for you. Some applications are health goals, looking for a new job, and helping you sleep or concentrate.

First, choose a pattern that appeals to you. You can either sketch it out on paper or use your imagination. I often use a star because stars are lucky to me. Some others that are common are circles, interlocking circles, a spiral, or a triangle. Choose something that resonates with you and your intent.

Next, find stones that reinforce the intent that you want to push forth. Consider this a battery for your magical spell.

Let's say you're making a grid to help you concentrate on studying for finals. We'll start this crystal grid during the full moon. Draw or imagine the shape of the grid that you'll be using, and decide which stones are best for concentration and studying. Let's use sodalite and lapis lazuli.

Find other things that might add a little "you" to the grid, such as jewelry, flowers, or shells. One of my favorite things to use is a robin eggshell that I found that brings so much potential to the grid. I put it in the center of most of my grids.

Clean your crystals. You can use smoke from an herb bundle or incense or run them under water.

Write your intent to remain calm and focused during your finals. Write what will happen when this occurs: you'll get excellent grades and succeed in your goals. You will approach your finals with confidence, and everything will work out the way you need it to. While you're writing, visualize what you want to happen. Imagine yourself sitting calmly in class, answering questions with authority, and then leaving the final feeling excited and successful.

Place the note in the center of your grid and place your crystals in the pattern you decided upon. Leave the grid in place until the next full moon. If you need to start your grid outside the full moon, that's fine. The moon is full somewhere at all times. Just adjust the spell as you need to.

Now, there was a time in my life when I definitely did not have a dozen pieces of labradorite or any other crystal or specific flavor of rock. That's okay. You can go into the yard and find pebbles or stones or pinecones or sticks that can hold the energy for you. Don't let lack of supplies keep you from your magic. You can also write the stone name on paper and place it in the grid. The universe gets you and what you're trying to do.

If you're going to keep your grid private, you can create it online by copying and pasting images of the stones in a pattern and saving the document. Be creative. Make the spell work for you as best as you can.

CANDLES

Candles provide a focus. If you are meditating, you can stare at the flame to take your mind to a very calm place. Bringing light to your magic is a ceremonial step that helps set the boundary of your spell crafting, and it can be a very distinct marking of the beginning and the end of the work: light the candles when you start, and blow them out when you're finished.

Lighting the candle or incense will hold space for your prayers for the time they're lit. I like using bodega candles because they'll burn for days. When I see them burning, they'll remind me of the work that I'm doing and that it's still out there. If I light a candle for a person, that intention drifts up with the smoke and goes out to whomever or whatever in the universe catches good intentions.

Candles are a part of nearly every tradition in nearly every religion. Particularly in the wintertime, when things are dark and still, brilliant points of light touch every heart and every faith. Lights that burn through the night give us all hope for the coming spring. Every time a candle is lit, a little bit of hope goes out into the universe. Even if it's just a little hope of a sweet smell to keep you company during the day or a big hope that your prayers will reach those that you love who have died.

The colors of the candles can help bring another level of energy to your magic. I would recommend keeping a stash of candles on hand. You can get a gross of white tea lights and a selection of taper or votive candles in whatever colors you like. I prefer soy or beeswax candles because they're natural, but you can use what's most readily available for you. I generally use white candles because I feel like white is a clean slate to start with, but here are different colors and meanings for your candle work:

Red: Any powerful emotion, such as rage, love, protection

Orange: Creativity, adventures

Yellow: Healing, intellectual clarity

Green: Growth, healing, prosperity

Blue: Health, calm, mental health, communication

Purple: Expanding wisdom, expanding influence

Black: Removal of negative energies, breaking bad habits, cord cutting

White: Healing, any other intent

You can time your rituals using the moon and choose the color or colors that closely align with your intent. While I'm preparing for the spell, I make sure that I have time to create the space to channel my energy into the candle. The candle is a vehicle for your intent.

INCENSE

Incense changes the energy of the room and makes it a sacred space, whatever sacred means to you. When I light a certain incense, I'm in the headspace to write. When I light another, it reminds me of my grandmother, and I usually clean the house or hang out with my kids at this time. Scent memory is very strong and can tie you easily to another place or time. If I smell dragon's blood incense, it's 1978 and I'm in my grandma's kitchen, helping her peel potatoes and listening to Patsy Cline.

I love incense for hitting a reset button in my mind. I am very affected by smell and have found that something as simple as changing the air around me will change my entire mood and focus. If you find yourself in need of a shift in composure, incense works quickly and can be used for a blessing or cleaning of your space. Incense comes in sticks, cones, and loose powder. You can find charcoal incense and natural blends.

Incense in magic can be used to home in on the intent that you're setting. By enhancing the intent, you shift the energy in the room and get yourself in a better state of mind. It can create a sense of calm and help create a clear starting point for your work.

Here are some types of incense and the energy they put forth:

Amber: Love, happiness

Bay: Psychic energy, predictive dreams

Cedar: Psychic energy, prevent nightmares

Cedarwood: Healing, purification, prosperity

Copal: Purification, protection

Dragon's Blood: Purification, sexual potency

Frankincense: Increase positivity, purification, protection

Jasmine: Prosperity, love

Lavender: Relaxation, sleep

Lemongrass: Concentration

Mint: Prosperity, healing

Patchouli: Prosperity, love

Rose: Courage, fertility, love

Sage: Protection, purification[14]

Sandalwood: Clearing negative energy, astral projection

Sweetgrass: Calling ancestors for guidance

Vanilla: Love, sex

Yarrow: Courage

Ylang-Ylang: Love, prosperity

OILS

Oils have been used as part of magical practice since before recorded history. Frankincense and myrrh are both featured in the Christian Bible, as well as oil used for anointing bodies. Jesus washed people's feet with oil, anointing them. Oils were found in ancient China and Africa, including Egypt. They contain the energy of the plants from which they were made and lend that energy to us.

If you were walking toward a goal—your spell—any signs or arrows that could help you hit the target would help, right? This is what oils can do for your magic. They nudge the energy even further in the direction you're pointing. They also smell amazing, and smell has immense control over our moods and focus. They enhance our natural inclinations and can direct us toward the correct state of mind for a particular spell. Simply apply oils to your petitions, candles, or cords. Oils can be used for nearly every purpose as well. Love, prosperity, road opening—you name it.

---

14. Research sage before using it to decide if it is appropriate for you to do so. White sage use is problematic due to cultural appropriation, and the plant is at risk due to commercial harvest of wild sage. If you use it, please be sure it is ethically sourced! You can even grow your own.

Oils are a part of sympathetic magic—using items to transfer the intent to you or someone else. These can be used independently or with other forms of magic to sharpen the focus and add a little oomph to the spell. You can anoint the candle, jar, or other item with the oils, or you can put them on your body or clothing. Oils can be used to mark your home with sigils, applied to petitions, used in your amulet pouches, or used to bless your stones.

If you wear the oil, be cautious of allergies, rashes, and burns. Do a spot test first to make sure it's okay to have on your skin. You'll want to store oils in a cool, dark cupboard, and be sure that you don't use them after they've gone bad. There is also a difference between infused and essential oils. Essential oils are more concentrated and therefore more expensive, and they should be mixed with a carrier oil before applied to the body.

You can make these yourself (but do your research first) or purchase them. I generally avoid the kitchen unless I'm reading cards, and I prefer to buy my oils in Nashville at Aromagregory, one of my favorite new age stores, owned by magician Gregory Lee White. This list of oils and their uses comes from his book *The Use of Magical Oils in Hoodoo, Prayer, and Spellwork.*

Love and Sex: Sandalwood, ylang-ylang, lavender, patchouli vanilla, jasmine

Happiness: Any citrus oil (excluding lemon oil, which would be saved for a spell to do with souring)

Power or Success: Chamomile, geranium, patchouli, anise, vetiver

Financial Gain: Ginger, nutmeg, patchouli, and clary sage[15]

---

15. Gregory Lee White, *The Use of Magical Oils in Hoodoo, Prayer, and Spellwork* (Nashville, TN: White Willow Books, 2017), 17.

I find that the most effective spells are either fueled by intense emotion or by approaching the spell quietly, steadily, and with your whole arsenal of magical tools at your side. Consider walking into a job interview. Would you wear jeans and a t-shirt? Would you sit in a relaxed manner or sit up straight and attentive?

Just as you would approach the interview, you should approach your magic. Lay your tools out in front of you. Light a candle or incense whose colors and scents enhance your spell. Apply oil that will give it a boost. Choose the right time of the month by the moon and be sure that you're calm. Move your body or tools sunwise (clockwise) rather than widdershins (counterclockwise). Yes, your magic will work without all these trappings, but it will work *better* if you use them.

OTHER COMMON TOOLS

There are a lot of tools that will help you with your magic. I know I'm saying this a lot in this book, but you really have to decide what *you* need and what *you* don't. Here is a list of common tools and how to use them. These are tools commonly used in Wicca and other forms of magic. I generally rely on my fingers or hands in place of a wand, so I've put in a thing that you can use in its place when you don't have or can't get the tool.

Tool	Uses	Alternatives
Wand	Focusing and directing magic	A pointed finger, your hand
Mortar and pestle	Mixing herbs used in spells or oils	Buy the herbs pre-ground

Tool	Uses	Alternatives
Ritual knife (athame)	Drawing circles, calling circles, pulling blood for spells	Butter knife from the kitchen; Grandma's old knife, sharpened
Jar with lid	Storing honey spells, potions, witch bottles	Ziplock bags
Tarot cards	Divination	Oracle cards, playing cards

CHAPTER 5

Magical Timing and Direction

Timing is another tool in your toolbelt. If the energy around you is lending itself to releasing things that get in your way, why not step into that flow and align your magic with it? I like to consider the things that I'm dealing with, write each challenge or opportunity down, and then see where it would best fit timing-wise. This is not an excuse to put off magic that needs to happen now. Rather, if you have the time, use it well.

THE MOON

About a decade ago, two friends and I decided it was time for us to quit smoking. We'd each tried traditional methods, such as going cold turkey and using patches and gum. We were all still struggling and still trying to quit. I invited them to my house to do some magic and give it a shot. We sat outside with four candles around us in a circle. We each wrote a note to cigarettes, thanking them for being there for us and asking them to let us go. We each had one last smoke together, talking about all the times we remembered bonding over a cigarette. Then, we burned our letters and leaned back on our hands, awash under the light of the full moon. We embraced it. We basked. We all quit smoking that night.

The strangest part of that night was not that we all quit. It was that we lost track of time. I thought we'd been outside for an hour. When we got back in the house, three hours had passed. We all felt giggly and full of hope and happiness. We all felt lifted. We absorbed that beautiful full moon energy and carried it with us for days.

You don't have to be a Pagan to follow the cycle of the moon. Some believe that the influence of the moon on humans is possibly hormonal and not gravitational pull as previously believed. Common practice is to observe the moon's cycle and time your spells accordingly. During the full moon, do spells that will bring bounty to your life. The energy of the full moon is expansive, welcoming, and generous. The new moon is the time to release things. Bad habits, grief, or crushes gone bad. This ebb and flow of energy is easy to tap into, easy to track, and an excellent way to follow the progress of your work. This chart demonstrates the basics:

Moon Phase	Energy	Types of Magic
Waning moon	Release, clean, donate things	Magic to prepare for a move, end a friendship, lighten your emotional load
New moon or dark moon	Reset, dropping bad habits	Magic to quit smoking, clean the house, bring down old spells

Moon Phase	Energy	Types of Magic
Waxing moon	Clean, prepare for bounty	Financial spells
Full moon	Growth, expansion, new habits	Focusing on one thing that you want to manifest this month

The waning moon is a time to pull things away from you. It's a reduction and release. It's good for starting a diet or preparing to leave a job. It's time to cut ties between yourself and people who no longer serve you. This is the time to pare down your life and discover how lightly you can live. This occurs during a period of about two weeks when the moon goes from full to new. The reduction of the visible part of the moon brings with it a more intense energy, more focused.

The new moon is when the moon appears dark in the sky. This is a good time for fasting or increasing your water intake. New beginnings are suitable now, and it's a perfect time to quit smoking or drinking caffeine or alcohol. Any harmful habits that you might have can be worked with now, but it's a good idea to find the root cause of these habits and focus on those as well. House cleaning on a new moon is a fantastic reset button for the energy in the house. Tossing out trash, clearing clutter, and reducing the amount of stuff you have makes space for better energy flow and also just makes you feel better.

The waxing moon grows to full, and it builds up and increases the strength and energy around you. This is a wonderful time to prepare for growth. Is there a baby coming? Are you expanding your business? What is your magic about? If it's about expansion in any way, the waxing moon is a good time for this.

The full moon is for growth. I want more money, more friends, a better job, and more robust health. I want to build on what I have until I have enough or more than enough. This is the time to call things to you. This is the energy of the wild ones and the loud thumping of your heart and finding it matches the rhythm of the world around you. The full moon asks you to become full as well and join it in lighting up the world.

This is a fantastic time to bless your house. With incense, candles, oils, or words, the full moon is a wonderful time to bring in cut flowers, make offerings to household gods or ancestors, have friends over for a potluck, and otherwise celebrate your home. Bless it with people and laughter.

SUNWISE AND WIDDERSHINS

The direction sunwise (or deosil) means to move and do magic in the direction that the sun moves, and widdershins means to move in the opposite direction. In these times when knowing where the sun is depends on whether you've gone outside lately, you can also consider going to the right (clockwise) as sunwise and the left (counterclockwise) as widdershins. Consider this another tool in your magical tool kit.

Keeping your magical actions in the appropriate directions for either making or unmaking can give you an assist. Making energy goes to the right. Unmaking goes to the left. If you are turning to the left, you can "undo" something negative that you've said or thought earlier, or you can wish away some bad luck. This is called widdershins, which is just a great word. While carving a candle, carve from left to right to create and from right to left to remove something from your path.

The words *deosil* and *widdershins* are old, old, old. There is a rightness about that. *Widdershins* derives from a Middle High German word that means "against." As in, against nature or rightness.

My friend Karin's favorite spell is the sunwise turn. In Scottish folklore, sunwise is considered the prosperous course. Druids used to walk around their temples sunwise, and others would walk sunwise three times around someone to bless them. When Karin mows her lawn, she goes sunwise around the trees and firepit. When she cooks, she stirs sunwise. When she cleans, she scrubs sunwise. I like the idea of such a simple gesture creating a blessing or protection, and it can literally be used anywhere

She also does twist-tie blessings in her kitchen. When her family finishes a loaf of bread, she wraps the twist tie three times around something in the kitchen and asks for blessings for those in her home. Health, prosperity, love, protection, grounding, an attitude shift—whatever is needed.

SEASONS

Most folks I know do a big purge in the spring and in the fall, sorting out paperwork, stuff for trash or donation, and outgrown clothing. It just feels right to do so. Spring cleaning isn't just something that your mom made you do. We have an urge to clear our nests after the hibernation of winter. In fall, we start stocking the fridge and pantry to prepare for winter. This is another natural cycle that you can embrace as part of your magic.

You can gain inspiration from the Pagan Wheel of the Year. This is a cycle of solar events and the midway points between them celebrated as sabbats, or holy days. Each equinox, solstice, and cross-quarter day is an opportunity to time your spells. Here are the basic correspondences:

Season	Activities	Sabbats
Winter	Scrapbooking, organizing storage areas, protection magic, gift giving	Yule in December
		Imbolc in February
Spring	Love spells, health spells, clearing out of emotional and physical clutter, prosperity	Ostara in March
		Beltane in May
Summer	Magical celebrations, family magic, luck magic	Litha in June
		Lughnasadh in August
Fall	Purging, witch bottles, protection, cord cutting	Mabon in September
		Samhain in October

Using these directions and the cycles of the moon can add your energy to the natural ebb and flow of the world. You can also use astrology, but I am a wee baby astrology student and have added some books to the reccomended reading list for you. Think of it as jumping double Dutch. You can just jump in, but if you work with the rhythms that already exist around you, it makes it easier to flow. Don't make your magic harder than it needs to be. The rhythm and directions will give you a boost, and you should absolutely tap into it.

ELEMENTS

Earth, air, fire, and water are the four main elements you can tap into in magic. An additional element is spirit. If you choose to work with the elements, they can assist you in reaching your goals. Each has a particular energy that you can use to push your magic forward. Again, like astrology, the moon, and directions, these are just another tool to help you add fuel to your magical fire. (Get it?)

For example, if you are feeling insecure financially, you can create a spell using earth elements on your altar and in your magic by using corresponding colored inks, paper, or candles. You can place some dirt or stones on your altar at the conclusion of the spell.

If you are looking for a cohesive form of magic that will help you, you can use a pentacle in your spell. This symbol combines earth, air, fire, water, and spirit with a circle surrounding them to show the control that you have over these forces in your life. This symbol shows our balance and ability to manipulate the world around us.

The following is a list of the elements and suggestions of ways that you can utilize them in your magic.

Element	Colors	Correspondences	Uses
Earth	Brown, green	Grounding, protection, home blessing, prosperity	Use dirt from around your house in a witch bottle. Sit outside for magic. Add crystals to spells.
Air	Yellow	Employment, clarity, meditation, influence, communication	Light incense for concentration. Breathe on your spells.

Element	Colors	Correspondences	Uses
Fire	Red	Energy, intention setting, protection	Focus on a flame for concentration. Burn old spells. Burn letters for release.
Water	Blue	Love, family protection, meditation	Add water or tears to spells. Clean and bless tools.
Spirit	Violet, white	Spiritual enhancement, contacting spirits	Use a pentacle in your magic. Draw or trace it with oil to show all the elements.

You can add elemental representation to your altar with feathers, cups of water, stones, and candles. If you have a specific goal in mind, pull together the elemental items that will help you move forward. Tap into the inherent energy that the items hold and use them to strengthen your spell.

DON'T WAIT FOR PERFECT CONDITIONS

You will be tempted to wait for the moon to come around and meet your needs. It is a wonderful form of Pagan procrastination: "I would love to get a better job, but I have to wait until the moon is full in *Cancer* because I need that water energy to balance out my fire energy, so I can just work this dumb job for three more months until it comes around."

Following the moon, the days of the week, and astrology is wonderful for timing your magic. They help narrow the intent and focus to a laser-point beam. I highly encourage you to study and work any of these into your magical plans.

It is not, however, necessary. You don't have to sit still until the moon is waning to release that ex who is still in your brain. There is no need to put things off, because the core of all magic is you.

And there are millions of moons in the galaxy. The moon is full somewhere, for someone.

CHAPTER 6
Magical Help

Whether you have, want, need, or recognize that you have invisible helpers in the universe is entirely up to you. While the word *angels* brings forward a religious image, guides, spirits, and ancestors are more secular entities. I believe in all of them. I'm not a Catholic anymore, but in that faith, the things that brought me the most comfort were Mary and her kind eyes and the thought that a guardian angel was watching over me.

As I grew older, that guardian angel became my grandfather or my grandmother. I still felt like I had someone out there I could rely on, but it was no longer a faceless fella who had huge white wings and hair like Fabio. It was the grandma whose lap I crawled into when I was sad, or the grandpa who held my hand when we walked to the post office together.

There are other spirits out there who might not be your blood ancestors but still have a vested interest in you. I think of these guys as a spiritual think tank that is looking over my shoulder all the time and whispering in my ear, "Oooh, are you sure about that? Okay. Welp." Think of them as Jiminy Cricket.

Spirit is sort of an all-encompassing term that covers anything that isn't in solid form and technically alive. This includes all guides, ancestors, angels, beings of the in-betweens, and things that you see out of the corner of your eye. It's most often used in the positive sense—"let spirit guide you," for example.

Asking for support during magical work is awesome, but it's important that if you're going to ask for help, it can't be the only thing you do with them. Honoring these spirits is important. You can meditate and say thank you, send up a prayer, leave them offerings outside or on your altar, or donate to a cause the spirit would approve of.

There needs to be a balance in all things. I have pictures of my grandparents, and to honor my husband's Mexican roots, we move them to an *ofrenda* during the month of October. I light candles for them and say prayers.

Sometimes while giving a reading, I'll "hear" what I'm meant to say next. It's not auditory; it's just in my head. Sometimes I hear spirits laughing when I say something funny or ridiculous. Sometimes I'll be giving a particularly intense reading and hear "Oooohhhh, snap" from them. We have our own special relationship.

REACHING SPIRITS AND GUIDES

If you choose to work with spirits, guides, angels, or your ancestors, be respectful. Be consistent, and always say thank you.

Here's how to reach your guides:

1. Go to your quiet space.

2. Find a meditation that works for you. I find staring at a candle flame in a quiet, dark room will get me there quickly.

3. Ground and center.

4. After reaching a peaceful place in your mind, ask your guides to come forward. This can be your departed loved ones, angels, or your guides.

5. Ask them their names and if they have any messages for you.

6. Thank them.

7. Blow out your candle or otherwise end your ritual.

You might have to do this a few times before you get to the right place. This is a practice, not a onetime thing. You can control who comes to you by using their name and by saying no if someone who makes you uncomfortable comes forward. Don't forget that you're in charge of this process. With that understanding comes control of the situation.

They might come forward and speak to you, or you might get feelings, smells, or signs. When you're in your quiet space, you can ask for lights, a certain bird, or a word to be a sign from them that they're looking out for you. Keep trying until you land on a signal that works for you. Due to my obsession with the Legend of Zelda video games, a lot of the time I'll hear "Hey! Listen!" when one of my guides wants to talk to me or get me to notice something. Whatever happens just after that annoying fairy voice comes from the back of my head turns out to be meaningful.

As you become more experienced with reaching your guides, you can ask for more guidance, for protection, and for suggestions or advice. You can ask them to be with you when you're nervous or scared. You can ask them to keep an eye on your loved ones. Your relationship with your guides is precious and individual.

SPIRIT BOARDS

There are tools, such as spirit boards and pendulums, available for communicating more clearly with your guides. We'll talk about pendulums in the divination section. Spirit boards are also known by the brand name Ouija boards and have kind of a mixed reputation. I've found that people who grew up using them and had *great* experiences truly love them and feel safe with them. I grew up playing with them at slumber parties. I did *not* have great experiences.

I remember being in a friend's basement, all spooky and giggly, and we asked the name of the spirit who was communicating with us. The candle that was burning next to the table suddenly flared up, and the flame was about four inches high. At the same time, the planchette flew off of the board and into the wall about six feet away.

A friend told me that at one of her slumber parties, the spirit board said that one of them would die that night. After much hysteria and everyone calling their folks to go home, she couldn't sleep for days. So ... I'm super wary of spirit boards.

I have used them as an adult, though, and everything worked fine. We cleared the energy around the board and put crystals on the table. My friend, who is a reiki master, did an attunement on each of us, and we were sure to close the session when we were finished. In my head, I consider any portal to the other side to be like a car in a bad neighborhood. You can pick up your friend, sure, but two other folks can sneak in the back seat without your permission or knowledge, so you need to be smart about its use. I have two boards in my house that have a handful of salt in the boxes with them to neutralize them.

You, however, might be like my friends who adore spirit boards. They see them as a fun and easy way to talk to guides or folks they've lost. They don't seem to have any problems with them, and I have a friend who collects them and says that she never has a problem with them.

Before you use any tools, check with yourself about your comfort level while using them. What you don't want to happen is using a tool because you feel pressured into doing it. Be sure that you can find your center and be grounded before you go mucking about in the otherworld. Be sure of who you are, what you want, and that your house and spirit are protected. *Then* you can have fun.

A typical session includes two or more people sitting around the spirit board. You place your hands on the planchette and ask to speak to a spirit. You can get answers spelled out for you, or it will go to yes or no. Be sure to close out the session when you're finished by saying goodbye.

ELEMENTALS

Elementals are nature spirits that you can ask for assistance in your magic. The easiest way to describe them is faeries. Earth, air, fire, and water elementals are all around us in nature. You can ask for their assistance with magics when you're outside. I am anxious when it comes to inviting elementals into the house; maybe I've read too many fairy tales about what happens when you make deals with the fairy world.

I like to call in elementals when I'm doing magic outside. I make it a casual invitation—not a bargain or a deal—but if any spirits of air or earth are around, I ask if they can assist me, and then I leave a little offering, such as some tobacco, a pretty rock, or a flower.

That's as intense as I like to get with elementals, but some find a deeper connection there. It is always good to honor the land that you're on and the spirits who share it with you. Recognize that you're not alone on the land and that they were here first. Learn the history of the land you live on and reach out energetically to see if you can feel the spirits that live there. Show respect and be kind. If you care for the land around you, it can care for you back.

PART TWO

The Spells

These spells were collected from friends, books, memory, experience, and oral tradition. I have credited where I could, but tracing the origin of some of them was impossible. I did my best. I honor the men and women who came before me and passed this knowledge on. I honor my ancestors. I honor my sister and brother witches and the struggles they endure. Each of these will help you focus your intent and bring positive changes into your life. I've also tossed in some superstition, because things get passed on for centuries for a reason.

CHAPTER 7

Luck

There is something in us that craves a more active role in how our life plays out. If we can influence it, even just a little bit, we feel more capable and more invincible. All these magics are things that you can easily find around the house and that were accessible to our ancestors.

It might help to think of luck as something you can catch. Think of the feeling you get when you see a falling star—"Oh! Oh my god, look! A falling star! Make a wish!" That's exactly what luck is. You happen into it, and once you catch it, you have to protect it against negative thoughts. My friend Sarah Kate said that people become luck magnets and some become luck bouncers.

Luck magnets are amazing. Luck comes to them, maybe as finding the perfect parking spot when they're anxious about being late. After that, they close their eyes to expanding and encouraging that luck. What if you woke up every day and said, out loud, "Today is going to be a great day"? What that does is train your brain to find good things to support that statement. When you're in that headspace, you pay attention to the lovely things in the universe, which helps lift you above the garbage things that happen. You're still affected by the garbage, but it doesn't pull you under. Once luck comes to you, nurture it instead of batting it away without looking for more.

Some luck is found and some luck is created, but all these magics are here to put a little spring in your step and help you along the way.

Luck bouncers always seem to have that wrinkle in the middle of their eyebrows. They seem to exist between complaints. "Can you believe it's raining?" they say, instead of looking for the rainbow. They expect all bad things to happen to them with this sour, dispassionate, expression on their face.

If you look for bad things, you will absolutely find them.

Embracing luck and optimism is not a half-assed "thoughts and prayers" ideal. It's realizing that being an optimist in this day and age is a political statement and a level of badassery that most should aspire to. It's being happy and looking up *in spite* of all the hard things that surround us and being absolutely devoted to the idea that you do, in fact, deserve good things.

The following are a couple of superstitions about how to get and keep some luck and turn things around for yourself. I was trying to regionalize them, but they all crisscross and are found in so many different traditions. These are all of our ancestors giving us tips for luck, for sweet conversations, and for protection.

FOLK MAGIC AND SUPERSTITION FOR LUCK

Carry an iron key in your pocket. Iron is known to keep away mischievous faeries, and carrying a piece of iron with you is a sure way to keep the fae from distracting you from your path.

Have a key that opens nothing? If the key opens nothing that you own, then the potential is endless. What mysteries and wonders lie ahead of you? To have a key that doesn't belong to a lock makes it the key to the world.

If you say "rabbit, rabbit" out loud on the first day of the month, you'll have good luck for the rest of the month. I have researched the bejeezus out of this superstition and had no luck in finding its origin. I can tell you that it's fun to try to remember. My kids and I shout it at each other, and it is really great fun. It's a wonderful way to start the month.

Hanging a horseshoe over your door is considered good luck. Hang it open-side up. This is old magic tied to the horseshoe being in the shape of the crescent moon and due to the faery folk's aversion to iron. If you have iron gracing your threshold, they're less likely to come into your house.

Every time you see a shooting star, your pulse quickens and you gasp. You close your eyes and wish for the biggest wish you can reach for. What a wonderful blessing.

Pull a wishbone while eye to eye with your cousin and snap! You get the biggest piece. Hell yeah. Make a wish.

Salt has a lot to do with magic and superstition. Throwing salt over your left shoulder cancels out the bad luck you get when you spill it. I've seen buttoned-up CEOs quickly, quickly, quickly toss salt over their shoulders and in the next breath call it a stupid superstition. Salt is used in magic for clearing energy, marking boundaries, and banishing negative spirits.

Shake a chimney sweep's hand for luck. This is an old tradition and could be tricky now, as chimney sweeps are hard to come by.

If a ladybug lands on you, you'll have good luck. To be chosen by one of these beauties is luck indeed.

Knocking on wood can either rouse the old gods to your aid or chase off negative spirits. This has also been adapted by Midwestern dads, who will rap their knuckles on their foreheads for luck.

There are quite a few sewing magics for luck. If you find a thimble, it's good luck. If you pick up a black button in your path, you've fallen victim to a curse. Dropping a needle is good luck, but I think finding it without stabbing yourself is even better luck. Finding a pin is lucky. I think also because you didn't stab yourself with it.

Seeing a black cat is good luck in England and is seen as bad luck in America. I'd like to personally shift this narrative to reflect the fact that black cats are smart and wondrous and delightful, in whichever country you are lucky enough to see them. I have four (Minerva, Shuri, Leia, and Luna—house panthers).

Crossing your fingers for good luck might come from early Christians blessing themselves and their fortunes or from the magic that lies in the in-betweens. Thresholds, doorways, crossroads, and crossed fingers—there is unlimited hope in the midst of change.

Holding your breath or crossing your fingers when you pass a cemetery will keep Death from seeing you. Much like Harry Potter's invisibility cloak, ceasing the signs of life or calling down a blessing will remove you from the attention of Death himself.

AMULET POUCHES

A few different cultures will use amulet pouches. In Hoodoo, they're called mojo or juju bags. Some Native American tribes, including the Crow, Blackfoot, and Arikara, call them medicine bundles. The point for these is to put some sacred or symbolic items together to both protect you and attract luck.

I got a reading before I went to New Orleans for the first time. I was told that I had too much fire in me and that I needed to find some water so I could regroup my energy and find some balance. Joe and I got to that beautiful city just as the sun was coming up. We drove nearly to the water and parked and sat down, watching the entire sunrise. It was one of the best moments of my life. We walked to Café du Monde and had coffee and fresh beignets. We started walking around and ended up in Marie Laveau's House of Voodoo. This is a pretty intense space, with lots of energies floating around and lots and lots of treasures on the wall. Every few feet, I saw a mermaid of some kind. It was so odd. They were everywhere, and it seemed as if I *had* to see them, like it was some sort of watery Where's Waldo? I saw a keychain, a tarot deck, a book, and a statue. I walked further into the store and saw a picture of *la sirena*. La sirena is a beautiful mermaid/siren found in the Lotería deck. I grabbed it, laughing, and reached up to the cashier to pay. Just as I did, he handed me a small gray bag with a mermaid charm tied to the top. "I think you need this."

I hadn't talked to him at all since going into the shop. I hadn't talked to anyone. I bought the amulet pouch and later on, when I opened it, I found a small seashell, a white feather, a blue stone, and sand.

I carried this little bag around for over a year. I carried it in my pockets, my bra, my purse. I would turn around and run back in the house if I forgot it. It made me feel calm. It helped me focus and gave me kind of a warm, delicious feeling that gave me confidence.

After a while, though, it started just feeling like a bag with stuff in it. The potency and energy of the amulets in the bag just kind of went away. I looked up what you should do with an ex-amulet bag and returned all the natural pieces to their elements. The seashell went into the river. (I'm landlocked. I'm sure the shell understood.) The sand went into my garden. The charm went into my charm collection, and I put the feather in a bird's nest in my lilac bush. It had done its work and was finished. I said a little thank-you prayer, and the best thing about this is it worked as magical training wheels for my luck.

How to Make Your Own Pouch

SUPPLIES

Small bag or piece of cloth

Charms or small trinkets

Knot spells or shambles (see page 140)

Herbs or plants that enhance your intent

Stones or crystals that align with your intent

Earth from somewhere special to you

Other natural symbols: feathers, snakeskin, fur, teeth, or nails

Nails

Pins or broken glass (if you use these, make sure the bag is thick enough so you don't stab yourself)

Your own blood or saliva (or that of your child)

Your own hair or fingernails

Figure out your intent. Is this for luck only? Is it for protection and luck? Why are you building this piece of magic?

Find a bag or a piece of cloth that you like and that will fit in your pocket.

Go to your quiet place. Light a candle and some incense.

Line up the items in front of you and ask them each to protect you. You might say, "Feather, help me feel lighter and fly
above my troubles," or, "Rose quartz, help me open my heart and
keep it that way."

Tie the bag or cloth closed with three knots. *Really* tighten
that bag. You don't want it to come open until all the energy is
used up.

Say thanks to the universe for the luck you're about to have.

When it's finished (and you'll know when it's finished), return the natural elements to the world, and the man-made ones
can find a home in your house.

Dos and Don'ts for Amulet Pouches

- Don't open it and mess with it while it's working.

- Don't give it away.

- Don't show it to other folks unless you can't help it. This is
  private magic that you create and feed for yourself.

- Don't use anyone's hair or nails except for yours and your
  kids'. You could probably use your partner's if you made
  bags together or had explicit permission. Things related to
  your kids lift your spirit.

CHAPTER 8
Prosperity

The first step in gaining prosperity is to turn off the scarcity mindset that a lot of us carry around with us. We deserve good things. We deserve to be safe. We deserve to have enough—and more than enough. When you do receive, you say, "Thank you. I am grateful. More, please." It is difficult to reset this way of thinking because money is often surrounded by family stories and feelings. If you grew up poor, you developed the mindset of someone who is surrounded by want. Combating this can often take a lifetime. Luckily, we've got some magic to help you out.

These spells and superstitions will help you get to where you need to be mentally so your wallet can be where *it* needs to be.

HISTORY OF YOUR RELATIONSHIP WITH MONEY

In order to rewrite your relationship with money, it's extremely helpful to *write* about your history with money.

Pretend that you're writing your memoirs or writing to a trusted friend. Start with your earliest memories of what it was to have money. What enough was. When you realized how your family handled money. Walking through your personal history with money will help you figure out any hang-ups you might have or shame or guilt you're still carrying around.

These are some questions you can ask yourself:

- What were your family's financial circumstances when you were born?
- When did you first realize that you were wealthy, middle class, or poor?
- What feelings surrounded your family's financial status?
- When did you start making your own money? How did you spend it?
- Were you taught to save?
- What has your emotional journey with money been?
- What will your new emotional relationship with money become?

For example, my parents never said that money was tight, but we knew not to ask for things that weren't necessities. We ate a lot from the garden and never went to restaurants. As I grew older, all the money that I made from my jobs was going right into my college fund because we couldn't afford college otherwise.

Go into more detail and write all that you can remember. Remember that this doesn't need to be shared, so you can be as honest as you need to be.

The next step is to write your future:

- What kind of jobs will you have?
- How much will you have in savings?
- What will your home look like?
- How will you teach your kids (if you have them) about money?
- How much will you need for retirement?
- What will it feel like to be in charge of finances, rather than finances being in charge of you?

Go on in this vein until you are certain you've fully fleshed out your future with money. Keep this money history/money future writing in a safe space so you can visit it again to see how far you've come. Also, I always advise people to find a financial advisor so that they know exactly where they stand and have legitimate goals to shoot for.

Having a rough relationship with money affects every single part of your life, and the relationship should be something that you look forward to having control of. If you use these spells, you should be able to check your bank account every morning without wincing.

TREASURE MAP

In *The Energy of Money,* Maria Nemeth discusses creating a treasure map to reach your financial goals.[16] Similar to a vision board, this is a visual representation of what you want your life to look like. It can be humbling, at first, to see something that seems so far away from where you are right now, but after you've

---

16. Maria Nemeth, *The Energy of Money: A Spiritual Guide to Financial and Personal Fulfillment* (New York: Ballantine, 1997).

told your inner critic to shut the hell up, you can start to get excited about the future ahead of you. When Jim Carrey was a struggling actor, he wrote himself a check for $10 million and dated it for Thanksgiving ten years in the future. He carried it in his wallet and ten years later found out that he would be earning $10 million for the movie *Dumb and Dumber*. This is a version of the treasure map that can take you right to the spot marked with an X.

Choose an attainable goal. Sometimes starting small can build up your confidence to build a map to a bigger goal. Either write out what your goal is or create a collage that shows how to get there. For example, I might write, "My goal is to make $500 a week doing readings for the next three months," or draw a picture of myself with a certain number of clients in three months. Cut out magazine pictures of money or the numbers that align with your vision.

Keep track of your income, and make sure that you choose a date and keep it in your mind. Check in with your treasure map when you can. I have mine hanging next to my bathroom mirror.

When you reach your goal, say, "Thank you. I am grateful. *More, please!*" Then, set another goal. Why not? You deserve good things.

MONEY ALTAR

On my main altar, I have a small dish. Every month, I clean it out and start again. This is my money altar. I have had money problems in my past. We grew up "welfare cheese" poor, and when I was a kid, if it didn't grow in the garden or we didn't help with the yearly butchering, we went hungry. We split Happy Meals for treats. I made stupid decisions about money when I was younger and not so young.

The first thing I did when I was tired of being afraid of money was figure out a way to actively participate in my financial life. I'm at a place now where I can confidently check my balance every morning instead of being worried of what I might find. This transition was really difficult because I'd gotten used to the idea that money was in charge of me, instead of the other way around.

I use my money altar weekly and clean it and reset it monthly. I do this because it's important to me to have contact with money, and it's easier for me to have a healthy relationship with it when I'm attentive.

SUPPLIES
Small dish
Coins
Dollar bills
Cinnamon sticks
Mint
Golden charms or trinkets
Paper
Pen

On the full moon, start creating your wee money altar. This can consist of whatever you have. I have used all the tools above as well as lodestones (magnetic stones), a robin's egg, and a business card of a job that I wanted. Every few days, add something to it. "Feed" it. Give it a coin, a trinket, some fresh mint. Write a note to yourself with the amount of money you want to pull toward you, and leave it on the altar. Always approach this altar with optimism and expectation. On the eve of the new moon, take everything out and set it aside. Clean out the altar entirely.

Take the coins and dollars that you added to the altar throughout the month and give them away—to your kids, to a donation jar at the library, and so on. I leave piles of coins around areas where I know folks could use the money. The intent here is to circulate the wealth. We all do better when we all do better.

At the start of the full moon, start all over again. This is something that your family can assist with. Also, I recommend a deck called the Money Magic Manifestation Cards, created by Ethony, a witch and tarot reader. This is a deck of forty-eight cards with wonderful statements, such as "I have permission to be wealthy" and "Money flows to me effortlessly." They can help you realign your thinking about money, which will help the rest of this energy flow.

After a month or so, take out all the coins that have accumulated during the month and either donate them or leave them where folks might find them. Put them back into circulation so more money will come your way.

EMERGENCY PIGGY BANK SPELL

This is a spell for when you need some money, right now. Be careful with it. Be sure when you're crafting the spell that you don't leave the parameters too wide. We don't want an inheritance—just enough to pay the electric *and* phone bills this month. Remember the Wiccan Rede, "an it harm none," if you follow it. We don't want to get this money at the expense of someone else.

Also, I've found that this spell works best if you do it *fast*. That's how quickly we want the money to come.

SUPPLIES

Coin (Silver dollar or Sacagawea coins are super shiny and
amazing for this spell.)

Green votive or tea light candle

Pen

Paper big enough to wrap the coin in

While you're executing this spell, think about the money ar-
riving and going into your account. Picture your balance going
up by exactly this amount. Imagine how relieved you'll be when
it gets here. Keep your mind on "when" and not "if."

Write down the amount of money you need. *Do not* go too
far over this amount.

Wrap the coin in the paper. Drip some wax on the paper to
seal it. Place this in your money altar.

After you receive the money, I want you to save up 10 percent
of that amount to donate. I don't care how long it takes you. It's
important to give back to the community that pulled a rabbit out
of its hat to help you. When you have the money, bury the whole
spell packet in the yard, preferably in a garden.

MONEY CANDLE

I see a lot of candles that cost $25 and up that work as money
magnets or improve your business. Some of them are lovely, but
I always wonder: If you're having money problems, should you
spend $25 on a candle?

Bodega or novena candles are those tall, colored candles in
glass containers that you can find in some churches and markets.
They usually cost about $3. For money magic, green is the way
to go.

These candles usually last a week and can burn for a long time unattended. For safety's sake, be careful and don't burn your house down. You're going to anoint the candle with prosperity oil that you make yourself. This is just another tool to increase the intent of your spell. Be careful with the oil—cinnamon can burn and oil can stain.

You can use this spell to attract a new job, pull in successful interviews, and shrink debt. This is a good spell for the full moon. We want things to grow.

SUPPLIES

Green bodega candle
Black permanent marker
Olive oil
Ground cinnamon

Use your marker to write "I am" statements on the candle. For example, "I deserve wealth. I am financially comfortable. I can pay all my bills. I will always be comfortable." You don't have to be able to read them; you know what you said.

Mix 1 part olive oil with 1 part cinnamon and draw this sigil on the side of the candle. This is created by combining the letters of the word *wealth*.

Wealth Sigil

Light the candle and let it burn until it's finished.

Say thank you to the universe.

When your candle is finished burning, you can recycle it.

FINDING A NEW JOB

When your old job isn't feeding you anymore or you're just up for a new challenge, finding a new job can seem like an overwhelming task. There are a few things that you can do to help you along with your chosen career path.

After you have an interview, you are usually given the business card of the person you interviewed with. Don't lose it. You're going to use it after you send your thank-you email to them.

This is a simple spell, but you need to hold on to your optimism both before and after. Speak about yourself in this job as if you already have it. Plan what your office will look like. Decide what you're going to spend your first paycheck on. Get to this place of confidence before you do this spell.

SUPPLIES

Business card from job interviewer

Orange candle

Olive oil

Ground cinnamon

On the back of the business card, write, "I am happy to accept this position." On the candle, use your fingertip to write the word *yes* with a mixture of 1 part olive oil and 1 part cinnamon, away from the flame. Place the card under the candle and light.

Then comes the action. Don't forget to follow up with a thank-you to the universe. Don't stop looking for other positions. Be smart about your job search. Get a professional to check out your résumé. Keep making motions toward finding a job (even if you're pretty sure you're going to get this one). Show the universe that you mean business.

☞ FOLK MAGIC AND SUPERSTITIONS FOR PROSPERITY

Finding a penny heads up is good luck, and so is turning over a tails-up penny for someone else to find.

Grow mint near your garden gate for prosperity.

Leave some money on the windowsill so money always knows where to find you.

Place some pennies in your kitchen cupboard so you'll always have money.

For prosperity, fill a half-pint jar with honey, seeds, beans, grains of rice, and money. Bury it in the yard by the front steps. This brings money into the house and keeps it there.

CHAPTER 9

Home and Hearth

A house is not the same as a home. A house or apartment is a place where people live. A home is a place where people live, love, create bonds, and feel safe. Safety is a huge part of this. If a person lives in a house where their parent or partner makes them feel unsafe, it remains just a house. Home is supposed to be where you can drop all the defenses and insults of the day and find immediate comfort. It's supposed to be a refuge.

I've lived in my current house for nearly twenty years. I've lived in it during a marriage that didn't work out, during my years as a single mother, and now with my sweet husband, kids, and pets. The energy of our home shifted every time a change was made. When folks moved out and when other folks moved in. When we lost a pet. When we adopted three black kittens and utterly outraged our two-year-old black cat. When we painted the walls or rearranged the furniture. Same house, different home.

Consider that if something as arbitrary as paint can shift the energy of a house, what magic can you do with a concentrated effort? If you're lucky, you can build the kind of energy in a home that makes everyone who visits you feel safe too. The kind of home where your kid's friends can be themselves. Where your friends can just come by and you don't feel the need to clean hurriedly before they get there. Where people will just check out the fridge and grab a snack without asking. This is the energy we're going for, and this is a goal for all of us. A place to feel safe, where we can breathe.

HOME BOUNDARY BLESSING

First, if you feel like your house has an animus (this is a vibe like there is a spirit or observer of the land that you live in), you can take a step to include them into your boundary laying. A good way to do this is to make offerings. Every day or every week leave some tobacco or incense or milk or honey or whatever out in the woods right outside your home boundary so that they know *you* know whose land it is. (It is not yours.) Just say thank you. You do not have to engage, meditate, or try to contact. Just say thank you, drop the stuff, and go home.

If you have a house spirit, you can do the same thing. You can leave small offerings in your kitchen on windowsills, or on your altar.

Do not, for the love of all things holy, name the thing. It's not a puppy. If you do, it's going to start paying more attention to you. You don't want that. You can respectfully call it the Other. The Old One. Your helpers. A title or description, not a name.

I had a friend who started blaming "Tilda" whenever something went wrong it their house. "Oh, Tilda knocked over the salt. Tilda hid my keys." After a while, stuff started happening all the time, and not good stuff. They'd see a small shape out of the corner of their eyes. They manifested Tilda and gave her a job. And boy was she doing her job of wrecking their house.

They called me after something bad was happening nearly every day and was driving them nuts. I suggested that they draw a picture of her now and then another of her with her *new* job. Tilda was getting a makeover. While they were drawing, they told the story of how her new job was bringing good luck and joy to the house and that she was a valuable member of the household.

It worked.

Ward (protect) your house. You can make a salt ring *all* the way around your home, including the yard and garage if you want. Whatever part feels like home, that's what you encircle. I never go in my backyard ever, but my dogs do, so it's part of my home. You're essentially saying, "This is my dance space; *that* is your dance space. I respect yours; you respect mine." You'll leave the offering outside this ring. And no, it doesn't matter what kind of salt.

You can ward your house with any element that appeals to you or all of them:

Air: Walk around your home with incense and "paint" the air with the smoke. Imagine the smoke creating a boundary around your home.

Water: Carry a bowl or cup of water around your home and sprinkle it in the corners. Visualize each drop of water shielding your house.

Earth: Carry four stones with you and place one in each corner of your home. Visualize the stones holding the corners of your house down and creating a boundary.

Fire: Carry a candle to each corner of your house and stand in the corner. Visualize the light filling your home.

Inside your boundary, you'll create a selenite and tourmaline grid. On every flat plane inside your house, put a stick of selenite. In every corner of your house, put a chunk of tourmaline and a small piece of selenite. Have the whole family help. Selenite enhances spiritual clarity and protection. Tourmaline grounds you, connects you to the earth, and helps align the energy of the folks that live in the house with the house itself. You can keep the selenite perched on bookshelves or put the stones in a small drawstring bag and use a thumbtack to attach the stones to your wall. They don't need to be seen. They just need to be in the corners and on the walls.

If you move, you can remove the stones while you're packing up and rebuild the grid when you get into your new space.

While you're doing this, listen to good music. Make sure everyone is happy. Ask everyone to lock an idea in their head that this house is "safe, happy, protected." This is a cleaner version of peeing on the boundary of your home, basically. Lasts longer too.

Clean house. You can do this yourself or hire a housekeeper to take care of it. Be sure it's a deep cleaning. All those bits that you kind of ignore when you do your usual cleaning? I'm looking at you, under the pantry and ceiling fans.

Use an ethically sourced sage or sweetgrass bundle to "paint" the room with smoke. I always start in the basement and work my way up. After each room, either light a candle or leave a light on in each room. Whatever is safest. Your family can help with this too. After you're finished, meet up at the front door, sage it together, and then slam the door. The thought during this process is "good energy can stay, and bad energy isn't welcome here." Be sure to let good energy stay, or it'll be an energy vacuum and those suck.

Focus on pushing the negative energy *over* your threshold. There is a reason I asked you to do the boundary laying and threshold blessings first. You've got to have a distinct line around your house, and your threshold needs to be reinforced so you can push that negative energy away from your home. Think of it as your version of Laura Roslin's airlock in *Battlestar Galactica*.

Afterward, repeat the house cleaning at least once a year. Do it after gross company comes over and after fights. You can just do upkeep room by room.

HOME PROTECTION

The first time I used protection magic, I was home alone in my new apartment, and I *felt* something watching me. I was on the third floor, and my window overlooked a bunch of trees, so it couldn't have been a person.

I kept getting this feeling, and while walking past a window, I saw something. I don't know what it was. It looked like a ball of dark energy with eyes. Kind of like a really intense hairball. I only saw it for half a second, but I knew that it was staring at me, I knew that it was bad news, and I knew that it was threatening me in my home.

Nope. Not today. I went into the kitchen, grabbed a fist full of salt, and threw it at the window, shouting "Fuck off!" And off it fucked.

Every house is not a home. There is a huge difference between a place where people live and a home. A home is a place where families are created—both heart and blood families. Homes are sacred, and the energy held within them is powerful. This doesn't mean that you have to have a family in your house for it to be a home. This just means that the love and energy that grows there makes it a home.

If a person lives alone, their energy floods the house and can fluctuate with moods and phases they go through. The energy in a lot of ways is an extension of their aura, the energy that surrounds all people and things.

Just as you can enhance your personal aura by taking good care of your body, mind, and soul, you can enhance the energy of your home by doing some "housekeeping" in the physical, spiritual, and emotional space that is your home. You can curate this energy and cultivate a safe and healthy space in which to live.

Bonus: The better the energy in your house is, the better you will feel, sleep, and deal with issues. If your nest is safe and secure, the rest of your life can get bananas without uprooting everything in your world. You have a safe space. You can breathe.

One of my favorite places in the world is the home of my friend Sarah Kate. This is where I write. This is where I hang out with my crew for coffee and tarot readings. This is the place that I come when I'm sad and need a good cry. This is home for me, even though I don't live here. It's home for several reasons. The first is that Sarah Kate, her husband, and their kiddo are deeply in love with each other. They love and support each other unwaveringly. The second reason is because their friends are always there and are always welcome there. I cannot count how many times I've dropped by at the tail end of someone else's visit. People just show up, and when they do, they're given food and drink and a comfortable chair.

The third reason is because it just *feels* good. It feels good to be there. It feels good to walk up the sidewalk and even sit on the porch. Sarah Kate is a witch and has wrapped magic around and through her house. There is love and blood and brick dust in this magic and you can feel it.

People are drawn to homes with good energy. They can leave their stressors at the door and just belong.

This is something that you need to believe. You can feel good energy and bad. It's a leftover instinct from our lizard brains. You can tell when people have just been fighting in a room—the air feels tense and hot. You can tell when you're not safe—your entire body rebels against being there. You know when you're safe because your tongue unsticks from the roof of your mouth and your entire self relaxes. Pay attention to your body—this is part of your magic.

There is a very cool *Discover* magazine article that talks about microbial auras that surround you and follow you around. Families swabbed samples from themselves for weeks for scientific study. Researchers were able to identify which people were in which home by using their microbial "fingerprint." Also, the microbes followed people to their new homes and were similar in people who had a lot of physical contact.[17]

So, auras. They're a thing.

Home energy has two parts to it: (1) the thresholds and boundaries and (2) the energy that's within the home. Thresholds are the gateways between outside and your home, so doors, windows, and garages are these thresholds to your house. They are actual, physical in-between areas that allow people and energy to come into and leave your home. Not that ghosts and spirits and whatnot are looking for a window to leave, but energy tends to follow the flow of use. We use the front door most often, so that's where the energy goes in and out most often.

---

17. Bethany Hubbard, "Your Bacterial 'Aura' Follows You from Place to Place," *Discover*, August 28, 2014, https://www.discovermagazine.com/health /your-bacterial-aura-follows-you-from-place-to-place#.VAEj4GSSy61.

Boundaries are the imagined or actual lines that surround your home—not your property, but your home. Let's say that you own two acres of land but never use your backyard and rarely go to the side of the house. If you were to draw the boundary, you could hug closely to the back door and sides and expand the front boundary to include your porch and the basketball hoop in the driveway that you play at all the time.

The boundaries around your home give the energy room in which to play. Think about a bubble. When you blow bubbles, the soap forms into a protective sphere around your breath. The boundaries of the bubble are the sphere of soap itself, and the energy of the bubble is the breath inside of it. There is no threshold because it's a frickin' bubble, and thresholds would pop it.

Imagine, then, a bubble around your house. This is your boundary line. Wherever you live, that is your boundary. Where your dogs go to play, where your peonies are planted, where your mailbox is—these are included. That place in the backyard where you mow and never hang out? That's not necessarily included. If you live in an apartment, your boundaries are super clear: the walls, ceiling, and floor of your home.

The thresholds are any way into or out of your house. Doors, windows, and (everyone always forgets) garage doors. The entryway used most often is the strongest threshold in your home and needs the most warding and protection.

Our thresholds are places of power because they're one of the places of the in-betweens. Not here, not there. A clear line that shows where your home begins and the rest of the world ends. It's a line of permissions. People don't breach your threshold with anything but good intentions unless they're not good guys. People come to your home to share company and food, to hug and love you, and to pet your cats. People are stopped at your threshold when they are not invited, not welcome, and not allowed in. This is a definitive space that affects the energy in your home.

The energy inside your house (the breath within the bubble) is affected by the moods and energies of the folks, animals, and spirits who live there. Pretty much everything that happens in the space affects the energy, but we're going to focus on the cleanliness, clutter, smells, and lights.

When you walk into a room after people have been fighting in it, you can feel the energy that the anger and words create. This is a good example of the energy that lives in a home. If the family in the home lives separately (Mom and Dad on their laptops, kids in their rooms on their phones), there are pockets of energy that are as individual as the people who live in them. If the family is close (shared meals, shared spaces and times), the vibe of the house is a mix of all the people's energies and is much more powerful.

When a friend has a new home, first, ask them not to bring their old broom into their new house. This will drag any "dirt" from the old house into the new. Then, bring them salt, so their lives always have flavor; bread, so they never go hungry; and water or wine, so they never go thirsty. You can also bring them a candle for the bathroom because … you know. (Thank you, Phoebe from *Friends*.)

An old tradition about a threshold is that you're not allowed to accept anything over the threshold. You have to take your pizza from the guy on one side or the other. Another is that you shouldn't cross thresholds left foot first because you could cross into the otherworld. This is a Polish tradition, and Polish folklore is terrifying, so feel free to take this with a grain of salt.

Guarding Your Threshold

In front of my front door sits a little fox. It's been there for about sixteen years, and you would never see it unless you were looking. It's sitting in my garden, pointing toward my front door. Its job is to guard. To thank the little statue, I clean it twice a year and make sure that it's protected from the elements.

To guard your home, you can use any animal you'd like that you've got an affinity with. Or you can use sigils to mark your door for protection. You can also paint your front door or use colored flowerpots to lend their energy. Try these colors:

Red: Joy and zeal

Orange: High energy and artistic tendencies

Yellow: Sunshine and happiness

Green: Prosperity and health

Blue: Healing and calm

Purple: Spirituality

White: Clarity and new beginnings

Black: Absorption of negativity and repelling unwanted guests

Brown: Being grounded

HAINT BLUE PORCH CEILINGS

In Southern and Gullah traditions, there are stories called "haint stories." Part ghost and part boogeyman, a "haint" is anything that would scare you stupid. Haints feature in any story your older sibling would tell you that would ensure that you never slept again. According to these traditions, haints don't like the color blue. Specifically, they don't like blue ceilings or doors. The color tricks them into thinking that the ceiling or door is water or the sky, and they won't come into your house. You can find many shades of haint blue, but if it's on the ceiling of a porch or the front door, it's going to haint-proof your house.

There Be Haints

Jenna Matlin is a Southern witchy tarot reader and author of *Have Tarot Will Travel: A Comprehensive Guide to Reading at Festivals as a Tarot Professional*. She's also a good friend and has a wonderful spell for clearing weird vibes from your house. This spell is for any kind of weird energy going on in your house (negative energy, heebie-jeebies, astral ne'er-do-wells) and basically how to kick them out of your house.

Pick up several branches outside your home. It is okay if you get them elsewhere, like a local park. Pick them off the ground; do not take them from a living tree.

Grab three branches thinner than a pencil. Once you have picked them up, immediately take them home and walk around your home, especially around rooms that feel especially troubled. While you do so, visualize that the branches are sucking up bad energy like they would water.

Once you feel that you have sucked up the energy or presence, go immediately to your back door (or any door if you don't have a back door per se) or a back window if your front door is in a hallway, and repeat this three times while holding the small bundle in both hands:

> I break your tie
> I break your spell
> I break your power
> Ne'er-do-well!

Then immediately break all three branches and throw them out your back door or window. As you throw the broken pieces, visualize that the ties that energy or presence had with your home are also broken. Leave the branches where they are on the ground. Do not pick them up. Nature will do the rest.

If a branch did not break, then you might need to repeat the process.

SALT AWAY TROUBLES

The use of salt in magic is so common that it's almost the magical version of the mitochondria being the powerhouse of the cell. It's used for purification and protection and is used in so many different cultures. Folks in Europe used to chase witches away with salt, which aligns with the Ozark tradition that witches don't like salty food and a person should be seen as suspect if they don't like it. It was burned in Egypt to protect from evil spirits while on a journey and can be used to draw a boundary line around your home.

You can use salt in the creation of a witch bottle and in the cleaning of a home's energy. On an altar, it can represent the earth element and is known to absorb or transport energy. This is my favorite way to use it. I mean, this and throwing it at boogey monsters in the window. The following Hoodoo tradition that I learned from my Italian friend is an example of the crisscrossing that magic does in our cultures.

If your house is feeling odd—you had a cranky visitor or there have been a lot of fights lately—you can reset the energy by sweeping the floor with salt. I use only salt, but you can use herbs and plants like lavender and rosemary to add another dimension to your magic other than protection.

Also, I recommend using a good broom, and by this I mean one that feels good in your hands. It needs to do a good job, of course, and also feel like it belongs to you.

SUPPLIES

Salt, whatever kind is best for you

Supplemental herb (optional)

A good broom or vacuum

There are a few different ways to do this, but I like the most straightforward way. Clean your house as entirely as you can. This magical cleansing is best done after a full clean, but a monthly half-assing is okay.

Sprinkle the salt on the floor, both carpet and hardwood, tile, or linoleum. Sprinkle it lightly if you've made this a weekly or monthly habit. Sprinkle it more heavily if your fussy aunt just visited with a headful of gossip.

You can choose to sweep the salt either out the door or into a pile in the center of the floor. I prefer the center of the floor. I put it in a dustpan and then immediately into the trash, and the trash goes outside right away. If you're doing this on carpeting, vacuum it up and throw it outside.

I always like to light incense or a candle after sweeping the floor. You can also put some lemon slices in water and set it to simmer on the stove. This creates a healthy vibe to replace the ickiness that was hanging around your home.

MOVING HOUSE

When you move, you have a great opportunity to start your new home off on the right foot. If you're able, try to get the new place cleaned and painted before you bring anything into it. Use the steps in the home boundary blessing (page 124) to bless the house.

Post-blessing, you'll move all your things into the house and get them arranged. Everything except for your broom. This is a bad luck item you want to chuck before moving into a new place. After everything is in its place, you can set up your selenite grid and do your inside and outside protection work.

You can leave behind most of the items that you've used in your home protection work, but I would recommend bringing along your sentry (animal statue), your selenite and tourmaline, and any other items, such as bells, herbs, and so on. If you've planted any protective plants outside, you can take clippings of these to your new place.

Please let anything that you've buried in the ground rest where it is. Digging up old magic is a sketchy process and can bring old business into your life again. Best to let it lie.

CHAPTER 10

Personal Blessings and Protection

Personal blessings and protection have the same goal. Their job is to wrap you in warm, strong energy so that you can move forward with confidence.

CORD MAGIC FOR PROTECTION

You know that thing where you worked with someone who made you feel small or talked to you like you were garbage, and every time you mess up at your new job their stupid face looms up in your head? Yeah. I hate that guy. Or the person you broke up with who inexplicably shows up in your dreams seven years after you dumped them and won't leave? These folks still have connections to you and those connections can be broken.

Love and hate are really strong emotions, and they leave leftover cords of energy. This doesn't necessarily mean that you hate or hold a grudge against them, but that when you're feeling the same way you did when they affected you, they zoom into your brain like a Dementor. It can be easy to feel powerless when you hit that energy level of shame or blame or guilt. Whatever it is that ties you to that person and the time and place they represent. So we're going to back away from this person, time, or place (I'll say person in the example) and push them out of our sight.

In most major religions, there is kind of a "you're rubber and I'm glue" theory. In Wicca, it's that anything you put out into the universe will come back to you threefold. In some Eastern religions, this is called karma, and the idea is that the actions you perform in your past and current lives will impact your future lives. Remember that your magical ethics are going to become the basis of your magical practice, and think about spells before you do them. Is it right? Is it fair? Is it necessary? If so, move forward.

Go to your quiet place. Light a candle and incense that calms you. Breathe in and out.

Find a piece of your hair (only your hair), thread, or string long enough to knot seven times.

For the first knot, picture the person who is threatening you. Imagine that their energy is no longer able to affect your energy. Tie it tightly.

For the second knot, picture the person who is threatening you and imagine them turning away from you physically. Tie it tightly.

For the third knot, envision any cords or lines that connect both of you breaking and pulling back into the person they came from. Do this slowly and deliberately. Did you love them? Pull that back in. Did they hold power over you? Send that back to them. Do you fear them? Pull that back to you and ground it. Imagine that it's going into the ground at your feet. Hold your positive energies and release the negative ones. Tie the knot tightly.

For the fourth knot, imagine that your energy or aura is thickening between you. Picture the person standing a foot in front of you, and thicken your energy until you can't see them anymore. Repeat to yourself, "You have no power here. Go away. You don't exist to me. You don't matter to me. You can't hurt me." Tie it so tightly.

For the fifth knot, use the wall of thick, opaque energy and push against the person. Imagine them getting farther and farther away from you. This is not to harm, this is just to create distance. Any energetic cords that still connect you will snap. Push them away until they're out of your line of sight. Tie it tightly.

For the sixth knot, pull your energy back and use it to surround yourself. Surround yourself in its warmth and turn it into a clear, colorful space instead of opaque and cloudy. Be sure it covers you from head to toe. Tie it tightly.

For the seventh knot, tie loosely. Imagine that your energy is going into the ground and dissipating into the air. Release all the anger and frustration that you've pulled together for this spell. Say, "Release. Release. Release." Place the knotted cord on your altar, and when you feel like you can let this (and this person) go without any malice or anger, bury it in the ground.

Release, release.

You might have to do this spell a couple of times. Some people really dig into us, and it's hard to excise them without pulling ourselves apart a little bit. Also, what if your knot breaks? Tie another. What if your string is too short? Add another. It's not always going to be perfect, but the intent is the important part.

SHAMBLES AND THE WITCHES' LADDER

The world is filled with makers and unmakers. You know the unmakers when you're near them. They make your stomach hurt. They hurt people for fun. They exist in our communities and in our governments. For every piece of darkness that an unmaker creates, a balance can be found with some light from a maker. In less broad terms, if you're having a bad day, you can make something—even a little something—to combat that darkness.

Sir Terry Pratchett, may he rest in delightful wonder, was my favorite author. In his Tiffany Aching series, he describes a creation called a "shambles." It's a piece of magic you can create out of items you have in your purse, in your pocket, or lying around your house. The act of creating something, even an ad-hoc dream catcher of sorts, is an act of magic in itself.

An example of a shambles is a stick, a string or piece of hair, and a ring, all tied together into a web. I've made one out of a gum wrapper and a key chain. It's a cat's cradle made of things that you create to make something, to protect yourself or your house, or for divination. It's also a lot like an old magic called a witches' ladder.

Witches' ladders can be curses but can also be a series of concentrated spell work for whatever you need. The goal is to weave your intention into the making, and it will hold your magic for you.

> *House Protection:* Walk around your home and collect leaves, sticks, snail shells, and so on and tie them together with a natural fiber cord. You can hang this from a tree on the property to catch bad energy coming toward your house. Be sure to use natural parts because it will eventually fall apart, and we don't want to litter.

Quick Calming: If you're out in public and become upset, you can reach into your bag and make a quick shambles. Use what you have. Napkins can be used to pull through keychains. Just binding two things together can help stir up the energy around you and give you a reset.

Divination: If you find yourself without a pendulum, you can create one. Anything that will swing freely from your hand can be used. You can also treat your purse or pocket like a charm bag. Decide what each item represents, and then reach in and grab the first thing that you touch: the wallet means yes, and the lip balm means no. Whichever you grab is your answer.

Building a Spell: You can also put feathers or beads into your witches' ladder. This is similar to a knot spell. For each item added, increase your intent and clarify your goal. It's helpful to set dates with this. For the first knot, visualize what your life will look like in three months. For the second, six months. Create it until you feel it's finished, using items that are meaningful to you. I usually keep these under my bed or on the altar.

PROTECTIVE SYMBOLS

The first time I heard about hex symbols was in the book *Seventh Son* by known homophobe yet amazing author Orson Scott Card. (Just get his books secondhand. Easy fix.) In the Pennsylvania Dutch tradition, hex signs are often six-pointed stars that are a representation of the Divine in nature. It's a protection for the home as well as just being beautiful. In the book, one woman married a super religious fella who didn't want her to use hexes, so she wove them into baskets, planted flowers into their shapes, and used other sneaky methods to incorporate them into her home.

I have a friend who does this with her own symbols. She draws stars and circles and lines until they click into place. She stops drawing when it feels right.

You can also use some Pagan symbols of protection around the house. If you have to hide this, you can be creative. You can weave or sew them into things around the house. You can draw them on the back of paintings. You can trace them with water on your walls and above your doors. You can trace the shapes with an incense stick in the air. There are a lot of ways to integrate these symbols into your everyday life without making yourself a target.

You can use these on notebooks, tattoos, or the bottom of your shoes. I think that drawing and using these symbols can help you lift up your energy and vibration and that of your environment. When I was in high school, I used to draw this simple protection sigil on everything to help me avoid bullies. It worked.

Triquetra Protection Sigil

Each time I drew it, I would pour all my feelings into it. All the fear and anxiety that high school gave me. All the hurt and anger. I would trace it into my shoes, on my skin, on my jeans, and in my journal. There was a simple prayer that went with this: "Please." Please let them ignore me. Please make me invisible. Please give me a voice if I need it. Sometimes you just need to hide away, and this sigil helped me do it.

These instructions are for visible hex signs and symbols, but adapt as you need to.

SUPPLIES

List of symbols that resonate with you
Something to draw with: paints, oils, water, pens or pencils

Make a plan. What kind of energy do you want in your house, on your person?

Practice drawing the shapes. Precision isn't necessary but it helps.

Use colors that will enhance your intent. Here are the candle color associations for reference:

Red: Any powerful emotion—rage, love, protection

Orange: Creativity, adventures

Yellow: Healing, intellectual clarity

Green: Growth, healing, prosperity

Blue: Health, calm, mental health

Purple: Expanding wisdom, expanding influence

Black: Removal of negative energies, breaking bad habits, cord cutting

White: Healing, any other intent

Start creating. Remember, these can be as simple or complicated as you'd like. Here are some examples of well-known symbols and their meanings:

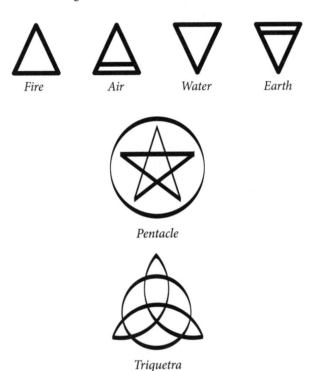

Fire   *Air*   *Water*   *Earth*

Pentacle

Triquetra

Sigil Building

You can create your own sigil by writing the letters of your intention down and combining them to make the sigil.

Intention: I want to find peace of mind.

Fewer words: Peace of mind

Fewer: PEACE

Combined: PEAC

Sigil:

You can apply this sigil by carving it into candles, writing it on top of spells, or drawing it on your body. I put money-drawing sigils on my right hand with ink when I need to. You can make the sigil a focus of your magic and walk away from it, knowing that it's still working for you. Recharging the sigil can be as easy as rewriting it.

Aidan Wachter, author of *Six Ways*, suggests thinking of the sigil as a seed.[18] You're planting your intention into the world. Be very careful creating these, because they can't be unmade. Use inks and paper that appeal to you and lend themselves to making the sigil special. This is your creation. Be careful with it, and also employ it smartly.

18. Aidan Wachter, *Six Ways* (New Mexico: Red Temple Press, 2018), 89.

PETITIONS

Petitions are written spells that you can use for any purpose. They're called petitions because you're asking your guides, your god, or the universe to intercede with you for a particular need. These can be as flowery or plain as you'd like. This is a conversation with you and someone or something that loves you. Choose your words with confidence. You can use them in tandem with candle work or witch bottles. I find that sicky notes work perfectly for these. The clearest directions I've seen for petitions were in Wachter's *Six Ways*. I've summarized and personalized them here.

SUPPLIES

Sticky notes (find a color that aligns with your intention)
Pen
Secret space to stash the notes
Ribbon or string to bind the intent

Write your petition across the note entirely. Then, turn it to the side, and write it again. Turn it a third time and write it again. Write it a fourth time after turning it again, and then write your name over and over on top of the writing.

Petition Image

Roll the intention toward you to bring something into your life, and roll it away from you to get rid of something. You can bind the intention with the ribbon and leave it in a box on your altar or stash it away somewhere.[19]

WITCH BOTTLE

A witch bottle is old, old magic that works to protect your home or the people who live in it. The tradition that I've read most about has its origins in England, but this is a kind of talisman that is common in nearly every magical tradition. You create a simulacrum for yourself and give it a job.

My family and I create new witch bottles every Halloween and burn the old ones. I've got one that my friend Karin made for me when I bought this house, and it's been in the windowsill ever since. This was how I knew we'd be friends forever.

She said, "Hey, can I have a lock of your hair?"

"Sure," said I, without even asking why.

I also have a few jars buried in the backyard. Apologies to future owners of my house.

The witch bottle pulls negative energy toward it instead of you. Think of it as a bad-vibe magnet. You place items from your body inside the bottle, as well as bent pins, nails, or broken glass. I always imagine that the bad luck starts zooming toward me, gets sidetracked by the bottle, and then gets sliced to pieces by the sharp bits.

Traditionally, you would use your own urine to fill the bottle, which is not the most hygienic thing. You can use vinegar as a substitute. You can also use nail clippings, hair, or blood to tie the bottle to yourself.

---

19. Wachter, *Six Ways*, 85.

If you use blood, please be safe. Don't be all dramatic and slice your palm like they do in the movies. Use a diabetic lancet or a sterilized needle to get a drop of blood. Be sure it's sterile and put some antibacterial cream and a band-aid on the puncture when you're finished. Dispose of the lancet properly, don't eat the blood, and don't get any blood on anyone else. Be a grown-up and be responsible.

Be sure all your materials can fit through the top of the bottle. Also, mind you don't cut yourself. (Although, that would kill two birds by getting your blood in there too.)

SUPPLIES

Incense or candles that encourage clarity of thought or
   protection
Glass bottle with a cork or other seal (found at craft stores)
Your nail clippings, hair, or blood
Any combination of bent pins, broken pieces of glass, nails,
   and bent safety pins or needles
Vinegar (or urine if you're down)
Wax (optional)
Red string

I like to start witch bottles on the new moon if I'm pushing something away and the full moon if I'm welcoming something toward me. I see this particular bottle as welcoming protection, so I start it on full moon. You can also use astrology or your religious calendar if you want. I make these on Halloween because I'm a witch, but again, your calendar is more important than mine.

The bottle can be as fancy or as plain as you'd like. I prefer clear glass, but colored glass is fine. The cork or stopper is really important. I don't have to impress upon you the image of a broken witch bottle a year in. Regardless of what you used to fill it, we want to keep all of it *in* the bottle. I have seen one that broke at some point during the year it was in use. I got the distinct feeling that it had taken a hell of an energetic hit for our family. Luckily, it was in a box, so we didn't have to get rid of the carpet that it was sitting on.

Go to your quiet place and light your incense or candles. Be sure that all of your ingredients are in front of you. It's best to do this in one go.

As you add the bits of yourself to the bottle, see them as you. Visualize that they're going to take the energetic hit for you. Thank them. Add the pins and needles.

Fill with vinegar to nearly the top of the bottle. Put the cork firmly in place. Optionally, melt candle wax on the join of the cork and the bottle.

Tie the red string around the top of the bottle and knot it three times.

Either bury it outside your home or put it in a dark place in your house, such as under the bed or in the basement. Make sure it's tucked away where it can't be kicked or found by anyone else.

Now you can either keep the bottle there forever, which is ideal for buried ones, or you can throw it out in a year and create another. I've found the best means of disposal are to recycle it in a bin or put it in a campfire. We have a firepit in our backyard that has lots of wee pieces of glass in the bottom. Be careful with it.

I wouldn't reuse the bottles unless you're feeling sentimental about them. If you do, be sure to clean them and then run them through a dishwasher so they get sterilized.

Remember to wash the outside of the bottle and your hands *really well* if you decide to use bodily fluids in this. We don't want anyone getting hep A because of a protection spell. Irony.

PERSONAL PROTECTION

When you were a baby, your mother or father probably kept the first tooth that you lost and the first curl that was cut from your hair. They probably still have it. If they're a witch like me, they probably have the umbilical stump from your belly button. Have you ever thought about this tradition? Have you ever questioned the keeping of your hair and teeth? To what end? Isn't that weird?

It's for your protection. Hair and teeth become a talisman. Not only are the lock of hair and tooth good luck charms for the parents, but they can be used in tracking spells and for personal protection. There are so many protection superstitions and spells that this may be the longest chapter in the book—and for good cause. We tend to trust exterior forms of protection these days more than our own intuition and abilities. What if we could "gear up" before leaving the house in such a way that bad luck went around us and danger didn't see us? These spells will allow you to walk and carry yourself in such a way that even if you do run into trouble, your confidence can act like a shield against the most annoying coworkers or the bad vibes that certain places give you.

Most people who are interested in magic and tarot and other witcheries could easily consider themselves to be empathic. An empath is a person who can pick up on the energy of other people near them. Sometimes if they're feeling vulnerable, they can think that it's their energy, or it can take their moods down to the level of the person they're near.

Building up this psychic and energetic protection can help not only in your magical work but also in your day-to-day life. You will start being able to examine the thoughts and feelings that are going through you to see if they are truly yours and if they are enough to change or affect your mood.

You can protect yourself in several different ways, including physically, emotionally, and spiritually. You can also increase your protection while reading for other people.

Physical Protection

After a long, long, long time of dealing with being *so sensitive* to the people around me, I've figured out some tips about keeping my energy separate from everyone else's, how to keep their energy from knocking the air out of me, and also how to keep other people from eating me energetically.

The first thing is basic health. If you're strong, you have better boundaries and are more grounded. Now, I'm strong-ish with my dumb asthma and bad back, but I have found that when I eat good food and go to the gym, I'm less likely to let other people's drama affect me. I don't read tarot when I'm sick, for example, because the readings are all over the place.

Second is geomancy. Keep some rocks in your pockets to keep you on the ground. I like labradorite and jet for when I'm feeling floopy. We also have a selenite and black tourmaline grid in our house that does some of the work for us.

I also find that washing your hands well after meeting folks helps immensely. Running water is fantastic for clearing away unwanted energy. You can also be sure that people don't touch you anywhere on your body where one part joins to the other. Elbows, knees, at the crook of your neck, your wrist—these places are favorites for energy vampires to start chomping on you. Once I realized this, I started moving away from folks while we were talking. This one dude always touched the small of my back and my elbow, and I felt like crap after talking to him. Once I stopped letting him near me, that awful feeling disappeared. Also, folks shouldn't touch you without permission ever.

Emotional Protection

I heard something a few months ago, and I can't get it out of my head. Someone said, "You don't have to believe every stupid thought that goes through your head." This resonated with me and I sat with it for a while. In my head, I heard, "You also don't have to feel every dumb emotion that goes through your heart."

Wait, what?

Just because an emotion runs right into me, I don't have to internalize it? 'Scuse me? You mean I've been flying off the handle for no reason?

If something frustrating happens in the morning, does it deserve to make your whole day miserable? Was it that big of a deal? Obviously, we're not talking about anything serious, but how can you tell the difference between an emotional wave and a serious issue?

I have four questions that I use to help decide whether or not to react to a transient feeling:

1. Is it yours? Does this feeling belong to you? Have you been around someone who's had emotional trauma, and maybe you picked up on that? Were you in a place that made you feel really low energy and haven't come back from there yet?

2. Is it important enough to act on or react to right now? Remember, you don't have to participate in every emotion that goes through your body. Do you need to act on this?

If your kid is being mouthy, can you correct them without becoming irate?

3. What are the long-term effects of reaction? If your partner drives in a way that makes you upset, is it better to put your hand on their arm and ask if they could take it easy, or to follow your first impulse and say, "What the hell is your problem? Trying to kill me?" This sounds like an overexaggeration, but sometimes empaths forget that other people in the room have emotions too and that ours aren't the center of the universe. I know. Shocking.

4. How long should you carry this? If it's someone else's, drop that mess. If it's not that important, deal with the problem rationally and then drop it. If you go through *all* these checklists and you are still upset, sad, irate, or furious, then honor that feeling and seek to resolve it.

The great thing about being an empath is that you're really sensitive. The bad thing about being an empath is that you're really sensitive. It's important to learn how to check in with yourself to be sure you're not being carried away on a wave of someone else's trauma.

Spiritual Protection

Picking up on other people's trauma can get really, really heavy. I always imagine it as a backpack. When I do a reading for someone, I have to be very careful to leave their reading on the table. If I don't, now I'm carrying two backpacks. If my partner is having stress, I put an arm in his backpack. Now I have two and a half. It's a cumulative thing, and they are layered in such a way that yours is always on the bottom and you never get time to delve into your own spiritual issues.

Either that was a genius analogy or made no sense at all.

Anyway, carrying all that weight can be spiritually depressing. Feeling responsible for other people's happiness can cause guilt and a feeling of not being good enough to help. This often snowballs into feeling like a failure because you can't fix the world. Anything that pulls your head down needs to be corrected. It isn't that you can't help other folks, but you can't live there. Spirituality is all about interconnectedness, but what happens when we feel like we can't connect in a meaningful way anymore?

The world is hard, yes. Recently, it's been absolutely brutal to folks who are already vulnerable, and our hearts break for them. Although we could become misanthropes and shut the door to the world, there are other options that won't leave us spiritually drained:

- Get off your phone. Seriously. Unless you can have a direct effect on whatever the daily trauma is, submerging yourself in it daily is useless and painful. If you want to help the families on the border, for example, find a charity that will directly help them and do what you can. Then get off your phone.

- Look for good things in your world. In your home, your community, and in the world. If you surround yourself with negativity, you will find it hard to keep your chin above water. If you deliberately seek out joy, it will help you become bulletproof to the ups and downs of the universe.

- Find a spiritual community, whether it's a mosque or temple or church or a Quaker Friends meeting or a meeting of the Rationalist Society. Volunteer with queer kiddos or an animal rescue. Find something that isn't about you. Spend an hour a week with like-minded folks who are trying to make the world a better place.

- Pray, in whatever way you pray, to whomever hears your prayers. Close your eyes and ask your higher self, consciousness, your god, the universe, or your ancestors to give your heart a break from breaking and trust that someone heard you. Take a deep breath. Take another one.

- Take care of yourself physically, spiritually, mentally, and emotionally. You have got to take better care of yourself when you're feeling disconnected. If it seems too challenging, start with the basics. Drink some water. Move your body. Take your meds. Eat something green.

Take care of yourself (first) and whomever else you can. We're all in this together.

PROTECTION DURING DIVINATION

Not surprisingly, lots of empaths are pulled to reading tarot oracle cards or other forms of divination. Part of being sensitive in this way is looking for tools to make the emotions you're soaking up make sense. I have very clear memories of sitting straight up in bed while all alone and saying, "Why the hell am I so sad?" Whammo. Sometimes it comes out of nowhere.

You are the most open to being an emotional sponge while you're doing the actual reading. With the cards, you have created a connection with the person you're reading, and the flow of that connection goes both ways. I once did a reading for a client without my cards. I held her hand, did the whoooole reading, and broke down sobbing on the way home. While I was crying my eyes out on the side of Highway 44, she texted me, saying that she hadn't felt so good in years. Mmmhmm.

How do you give compassionate, caring readings without taking on someone else's stuff?

- No touching. Do your reading without putting your hands or self near the person you're reading for. This physical distance will help you keep emotional distance from their reading. No touching until after the reading is over and your cards are put away.

- Zip it with the chitchat. Even if you're reading for a friend, try to just read in one shot. There should be a period of time that is defined as The Reading. Everything else should be discussed before or after the reading. Giving the reading clear boundaries will help you enforce yours.

- When you finish the reading, make a conscious effort to visualize closing the connection between you and the person you're reading for. Don't walk away with that channel still open. Don't drag them home with you. It won't be healthy for either of you.

- Say no. Again, don't give readings when you don't want to, if you're sick or tired, or the person who asked is an asshole, but you're just trying to be nice. Say it with me now: "I forgot my cards at home." You can also say, "I do this for a living, so I need money for it." Boundaries, boundaries. If you're feeling vulnerable before a reading even starts, you'll have a harder time holding firm to your boundaries during it.

Just remember that the reading is an exchange. You're getting paid either in your rate per reading or in coffee or dinner. You're not reading for free, right? Because we don't devalue ourselves like that.

In an exchange, you give something, and then they give something. After the exchange, you walk away with what you were given, and they walk away with the reading. It's not yours. It just went through you; it's not of you.

If you can remember the exchange part of this interaction, you'll do just fine.

SPELL TO PROTECT A LOVED ONE

Dedicating a candle to someone is a wonderful way to protect them. I would recommend only doing this for people you are related to or know for certain that you will not be separated from. Any magic done between people creates ties between those people. Those ties are hard to break.

For protection, you can choose a taper candle or a pillar in the color that reminds you most of the person. You're going to want something that you can carve on. Be careful with the blade while carving.

SUPPLIES

Taper or pillar candle
Utility blade or knife
Paper
Pen
Fireproof surface

Go to your quiet place. Imagine the color of the candle surrounding the person. As you sit quietly, start carving designs and words into the candle. You can use one of the protection sigils found in other chapters in this book. You can use the person's astrological symbol or any religious symbols that align with your views.

Words that you can carve can include *safe, protection, love,* and *embraced.* It doesn't matter if they're legible. You know what they mean. Say the person's name. Remember, names have power.

After carving the candle, you can write your intent down on a small piece of paper and put it under the candle. Be sure that you don't burn your house down, please. Allow the candle to burn down, and when you dispose of it, say thank you.

You can also use melted wax to surround the paper and keep it in your home, protected. I have a small box with the names of my loved ones and intents somewhere in my house. It makes me feel better knowing that it's there.

KEEP MY NAME OUT
OF YOUR MOUTH SPELL

I hate gossip. It sows seeds of unrest and spreads darkness and garbage. I didn't realize until I was in my thirties that people talked about me when I wasn't around, and I was so much happier. I realize that it was a miracle that I had wandered around most of my life completely unaware of my impact on the world, but it was really nice. One of the worst parts about gossip is that you feel completely powerless against it.

Well, you don't anymore. Let's shut some faces, witches.

SUPPLIES

Picture or drawing of the person running their mouth. Stick
    figures work.

Black marker
Fireproof dish, firepit, or metal bin
Lighter or matches

Go to your quiet place. Say out loud what the person said about you, and then write the opposite on their picture. Draw an X over their mouth.

Say, "You have no power over me." Say it as many times as you need to to believe it.

Put the picture in the dish or pit and burn it. Let the ashes blow away and take your anger and resentment with it.

BACK *OFF* SPELL

I learned this from my dear friend Sarah Kate. I had someone in my life who was damaging my calm and threatening my happiness. That had to stop. You're going to have a field trip with this one.

While you're doing the work on this spell, I want you to visualize all your hurt and anger going into the apple. With every clove that you push into it, imagine that you are sending bursts of rage into it. Your anger and rage are justified feelings. It's tricky to send that energy toward a person, but putting it into a simulacrum of that person can get the rage out of you without hurting anyone else. Visualize a wall of hot air separating you from the person you're banning from your life. Even if you can't get away from them physically, you can neutralize their effect on you.

SUPPLIES
Apple
Permanent marker or utility knife
Paring knife

Rosemary
Cloves
Salt

Carve or draw the person's name on the apple. Core the apple and fill the empty core with rosemary. Push the cloves into the apple until the name is obscured.

Field trip! Take that poison apple to the closest running water that you can find (river, ocean, etc.). When you get there, ask the universe to help you rid yourself of the taint and darkness that this person has brought to your life. Throw the apple as hard as you can and be free of it.

After you throw the apple, get your salt out and wash your hands with it.

Clap your hands three times. Be finished with this person. Walk away free.

REVENGE

This is a little tricky, as doing magic toward another person can be ethically questionable, but my theory about revenge is that if the connection between you and the person who hurt you is still open, you might as well use it. If they send good energy toward you, they'll get good energy back. If they try to get at you, well, what goes around comes around. Don't start nothin', won't be nothin'.

I had a situation with someone who hurt me. We'll call them Dick. Dick took my trust and hurt me, and then kept hurting me by spreading rumors and poisoning my friend's minds with lies about me. I didn't want to be the bad guy in the situation, so I tried not to gossip or cause problems. Being nice is completely worthless, you know? Nice doesn't help. Nice is a wet noodle.

Kind, as described by my friend Sara Benincasa, means that you have boundaries and so do other people. You enforce yours and they enforce theirs. So here I was, being nice and watching this poison spread. I don't think so.

The idea of this spell is to send energy back to the person using the connection between you, as well as sending some fire along after to burn the connection away.

SUPPLIES

Paper

Pen

Mirror, the same size or bigger than the paper

Black cloth

Black candle (we're looking for an ending here)

Go to your quiet place. You don't want to do this spell filled with emotion. You don't want to hurt the person; you just want to send their energy back to them and get it off you. We don't send hate back because that just begins the dance again. You send energy to them, they deal with it, they send some back. It's an eighth-grade dance of emotional energy, and you don't need it.

Write down everything that this person has done to you. This includes things that they've told other people about you. Write how it made you feel and the fear that it created in you. Write all of this on one side of the paper. We're not sending back anything that didn't originate with them. My favorite curse is "I hope the world treats them the way they're treating the world." You're handing their stuff back to them.

When you're finished, put the paper writing-side down on the mirror. Wrap it with the black cloth. Light your candle and place it on top of the covered mirror. Be sure that it's clear of anything that might catch fire. As you do this, I want you to imagine that all those words are going back to the person through the cord that ties you. Send all the feelings that were caused back to them. Release yourself from the anxiety and allow it to flow out to its creator.

Do not send any extra energy to them. Not hate, not rage, not anything damaging. Just what was handed to you. Hand it back.

When you're finished, imagine a spark of light starting at your end of the cord between you. Watch it burn until it's outside your house, then stop. What happens outside your boundaries isn't important, because you've been released from it.

Bury the mirror in your garden, at least a foot down.

Then comes the hard part. Forget about it. Forget about the person and forget about the poison. Work on healing yourself and moving on. Be sure that you put this to bed and stop carrying it around with you. Do not engage with them. Remove them from your mind, phone, social media, and life as much as you can. Breathe.

FREEZE!

You know that person at work who makes you completely insane in a million different ways? Or the ex-partner who continues to enter your life uninvited because you share a friend group? Or the sibling who keeps causing problems with their gossip? All these folks have something in common: you can't separate your life from theirs without causing a huge disruption. You also can't stand them and need to get to a place where being near them doesn't affect you so much. Ignoring isn't always an option, so here's a small spell to help them stop wanting to engage with you.

SUPPLIES

Paper

Pen

Ziplock bag

Water

Salt

Freezer

Write their name down, their full name if you know it. Put the name into the ziplock bag and fill the baggie with water and salt. Toss the baggie in the back of your freezer and leave it there.

That's it. That's the spell. No meditation needed. Just toss them in the freezer and "freeze" any annoyances that might come from them. What you're doing with this spell is suspending their energy before it hits you. It also introduces a little bit of "dead to me" in *your* energy. If they're frozen away from you, you're less likely to rise to baiting or annoyances. You'll keep cool when they're around. (See what I did there?)

FORGIVENESS

No one seeks to forgive, unless the burden of the old pain is bending them in half. Forgiveness presents itself as something that we *should* do. We can be the bigger person and forgive and forget. It's harder than that, though. I wonder if the blanket statement of "forgive and forget" isn't dismissive of your right to have feelings. Is there a limit to forgiveness? How bad is too bad?

There comes a time when, regardless of what was done to you, holding on to the resentment and anger is doing you more harm than good. It's not for the other person; it's for you.

SUPPLIES

Colored pen
Picture of the person
Paper
Black pen
Lighter
Fireproof vessel
New plant

Using the colored pen, write everything you'd like to say to them on the back of the picture. If you need more space, use the paper. Get it all out.

When you're finished writing, go to your quiet place. You might even take a walk or something to cool down before you start the next piece.

Now that you're calm and collected, go over your writing again. For each sentence, find something positive that their behavior brought to your life. Maybe meeting them brought a new person who became a valued friend into your life. You discovered how resilient you are because of them. You found strength that you didn't know you possessed. Whether they intended to make your life better or not, these are the gifts that you received because they were in your life.

Write what your gift was with the black pen over the colored writing, even if the only thing you can think of is *freedom*. Write it as large as you can. Cover up the other writing.

Burn the paper and the picture in a fireproof vessel. Watch them turn to ash. Remember who you were before you met this person and who you have become. Release the anger that you hold in your heart. Release the burden of pain.

At the base of your new plant or tree, dig a small hole in the dirt and bury the ashes. Allow the remains of this pain to help something grow.

I AM SO ANGRY SPELL

Do you know those times when life goes sideways and the rage you feel is real? You want to hurt someone. You want to throw things and scream. You want to use all the swears, and to make it worse, you're so angry you're *crying*. Oh, the rage.

What can you do? You can't hurt people. I mean, you can, but I think it's a terrible idea. It always comes back to make everything worse, and it's never as satisfying as you think it is. Let's decide that we're not going to hurt anyone, including ourselves. But we still have that rage. You have to figure out what to do with it and where to put it.

This spell will help you channel it and release it without hurting anyone. Ignoring anger is useless and unhealthy, and letting it build up gives it a chance to fly out of your face undirected and hurt people that you're not angry with. We're going to fire it out of us like that one time when Iron Man channeled Thor's lightning to lay the smackdown on Thanos.

SUPPLIES
Black permanent marker
Glass jar, preferably a mason jar (do *not* reuse this jar)
3 small glass jars or shot glasses
Eye protection

Fuck your quiet place. Just be mad.

Use the marker to write everything you want to say to the person or thing that made you angry on the glass jar. Use all the bad words.

Write one word on each of the small jars: *I am done.*

Find an industrial-sized dumpster. If you feel comfortable, scream as loud as you can as you smash the glass jar into the dumpster. Really put your back into it.

In order, throw in the other three jars: *I—am—done.*

As you throw them, live in each word. Let it resonate as ownership of who you are and where your boundaries lie. Scream a little more. It feels good.

After you're finished, go take a shower or go swimming. Get dressed in comfy clothing and get snuggled in. Release, release, release.

HONEY JAR

I learned this wonderful spell from Briana Saussy, who is the author of a wonderful new book called *Making Magic*. I learned this spell several years ago when I was going through a rather dark time and needed a little sweetness in my life. I needed to start noticing the good things in my life rather than the dark.

Honey jars can be created with actual honey but often are a little neater with sugar. I prefer raw sugar—seems a little closer to the earth that way. You can also use agave or molasses. Anything that will sweeten your life.

These jars of lovely magic promote harmony and love and can help influence other folks to look upon you and your life with a kinder eye and a sweeter heart. This is a form of sympathetic magic, similar to a traditional poppet or voodoo doll. In sympathetic magic, you are making a connection between a person and an item, and the magic that's done and surrounds the item is also going to surround the person. It's like the witch bottle, except instead of urine and rusty nails, we get to use flowers and sugar.

You can make honey jars for yourself so that you won't be as cranky at work or toward your loved ones. You can make them for your loved ones so that they can be happier and more compassionate.

Real talk? You can also make them to get your boss to stop treating you like trash or encourage a bank to approve a loan that you need. You are not casting magic on the person; you are aiming for that person's *feelings* toward you and how they act on those feelings.

SUPPLIES

Paper

Pen

Jar with a lid

Honey, sugar, flowers—anything sweet and natural

Candle

First, you need to write a petition. The format that Briana suggests for your petition is this:

> The petition made for a honey jar tends to follow a specific format. First, you will write the name of your target (the person you would like the honey jar to effect), then you will turn the paper 90 degrees and write your name on top of the target's name. If you are doing a honey jar on yourself then you do not have to do this second step.
>
> Some people like to use pencil for the target's name and then a pen or permanent marker for their own name—the idea behind this is that permanent ink is "stronger" than a pencil (which can be erased) and therefore exerts more influence. I personally like a strong ink that I can see well for

both names. After the names have been inscribed it's time to create a magical circle around them like this:

During the writing in a circle around the names, the pen cannot be lifted from the paper and this is why it makes sense to use a short and sweet prayer. I used the prayer: "love and blessings" over and over again.[20]

When you're finished, you can use oil on it and fold it. Put it in the honey jar and put a lid on it. This lid needs to be fireproof, so be sure it can take a candle's weight and heat.

Add your sugar and any other natural items that are of the same vibe. Cinnamon, flower petals, vanilla—whatever appeals to you. Be sure that the petition is entirely covered by these things.

Choose a candle that you like that can rest on top of the jar. I like using tea lights, as they won't melt down and will burn away safely. You can use a candle that will melt over the jar, but again, please be careful.

When I feel the need to re-up the spell, I light another candle. Some of them I've had for years. I consider that I am nurturing them and their intent as much as I'm nurturing the folks that I love. I keep the jar until it feels like its zip has faded away. I use all-natural ingredients so that I can return them to the earth when it's finished.

IMAGE MAGIC

Image magic is most well-known as voodoo dolls. You create a poppet, or a doll, in the image of a person and then use sympathetic magic to enact a change on that person. In this spell, the

---

20. Briana Saussy, "How to Make a Honey Jar (with Pictures!!!)," BrianaSaussy .com, accessed February 25, 2020, https://brianasaussy.com/how-to-make -a-honey-jar-with-pictures/.

person is you. Remember that with any magic, any spell that is connecting you to another person will create bonds, so be careful.

You can also use a photograph or a stick figure drawing that can create the link that you need between an item or a person. Sympathetic magic relies heavily on intent. Since we want to err on the side of kindness, I don't recommend using any image magic for nefarious ends or without explicit consent unless it's a softening of feelings that already exist.

You can use image magic in most of these spells. For example, with the honey jar, you can put a drawing or a doll in the jar with the rest of your ingredients. For petitions, you can write your words on a photograph or on a doll.

Since these are active magic objects, you can't just chuck them in the recycling and be done. If you've used image magic in any sort of spell, it's best to bury it far from your house with a small offering such as coins or flowers and leave it behind. Find a quiet spot near a stream or river, bury it, and walk away.

FOLK MAGIC AND SUPERSTITIONS FOR PROTECTION

Never cross a mushroom ring, or the fairies will come for you.

Fill an onion with pins to protect yourself from attack.

Paint the front porch haint blue to confuse the devil.

Use pepper for self-defense. Sprinkle it on the front porch to keep people away. Put it under company's chairs to keep them from staying too long.

Plant peppermint in the garden for protection.

Red brick dust brushed into the threshold or front steps keeps the nasties away.

Sprinkle salt across thresholds or windowsills to keep out evil spirits.

Tying a red ribbon around the wrist wards off evil.

Carry a piece of lightning-struck wood for protection.

Wearing the evil eye symbol will turn away evil itself.

Garlic, salt, and rosemary together cast away evil.

Knocking on wood brings luck and protection.

Hanging bells in corners will drive away negativity.

Braided onions hung over a door protect your home.

Use cloves to ward off attack.

Draw a cross in the dust outside your home to protect you and your home.

Uncross your knives to stop a quarrel.

Washing the glass of the front door with lemon juice lets you see clearly the intentions of whoever comes to the door.

Wear blue for protection.

A horseshoe upright over a door keeps the faeries away and brings in luck.

Iron nails over the door ward off the fae.

Knocking on a door three times deters ghosts (and summons Penny).

To cure a headache, place a bit of salt on your head.

CHAPTER 11
Love and Healing

We all know that you can't make someone do anything, especially fall in love with you. What you *can* control is yourself and the energy around you. This is not one of those "love and light" sentiments. This is not about loving yourself before looking for a relationship. Don't get me wrong, I love RuPaul, who at the end of every episode of his *Drag Race* says, "If you can't love yourself, how the hell you gonna love someone else?" I think this is not the most helpful sentiment. Some folks learned how to love themselves by loving others.

KNOT MAGIC FOR HEALTH

This is not about losing weight. This is about feeling good.

For this spell you'll need a string, a thread, or a piece of your hair long enough to tie into three knots, spaced out. It'll look like this:

Knotted String

SUPPLIES

Pen

Paper

String, thread, or hair

Yellow or orange candle

Cedarwood or sage incense

Go to your quiet place. Create the energy you need to feel good.

Write three habits that you need to change to be the healthiest version of yourself.

Here's an example:

Three Habits That Need to Change

1. Eating fast food

2. Not exercising

3. Repeating garbage thoughts/words about self

Write three things that you can do to change those habits.

Taking the thread in your hands, either think or talk about when you started these habits and why they continue. This isn't to blame or shame. This is so that we can realize that these habits didn't spring up overnight and they're not going away overnight. We need to honor what you've been through. Understand that we're not trying to kick your ass into health. We're trying to enhance the amazing creature that you are. If you were trying to grow a plant, you wouldn't withhold water and scream at it. You would cultivate and care for that plant. You would love it until it loved itself enough to make itself healthy, right? You're the plant in this scenario.

Following our example, as you tie the first knot (loosely— you're going to untie this), think of the things that fast food does to your body, how it affects your mood and your relationship with yourself.

As you loosely tie the second knot, think of the things that happen when you don't move your body.

As you loosely tie the third knot, think of what self-abuse does to you. It plants a seed, and that seed grows. Try to remember where you first heard those negative words. I'll bet you a million bucks it wasn't from you. The key to unlearning a habit is to put a name to it.

Next, untie the first knot—thinking and talking about what you can eat instead of fast food. Picture the food in your mind— what do you love eating that loves you back? Decide that by untying this knot you are releasing yourself from the unhealthy habit and making space for the healthy choice.

Untie the second knot, imagining what you're going to look and feel like when you're able to move your body every day. Even if it's just walking twenty minutes a day. Decide that your body is a tool and you're going to keep your tool in excellent shape so you can do the work you need to do. Decide that you are going to release yourself from inactivity and make space for activity.

Untie the third knot, create new words to say to yourself. Words that build up instead of tear down. I often suggest writing what you say to yourself on one side of a piece of paper and writing the opposite on the other side. Burn the left side and carry the right with you. Use it as a bookmark. Take a picture of it and use it as your screensaver on your phone.

Light a candle to hold your vision and some incense to carry it away into the universe.

When you've finished untying the knots, place the string on your altar or in a quiet place for thirty days. Practice the new habits that you've made space for. At the end of thirty days, reflect on what you've changed and whether or not it's worked. If it hasn't, bury the string into the earth and start again with a new string and more specific choices. If it's finished, bury the string and release all that energy back into the earth. Say, "Thank you. I am grateful. More, please."

TO OPEN A BROKEN HEART

I've had lots of tarot clients call me looking for love. Sometimes I ask them about their last relationship. Did you swear off partners? Did you tell the universe that you didn't need another one and that you were done?

"… Yeah."

Okay. Did you tell the universe you changed your mind?

You gotta do that. You have to make your intentions well known when they change. Think about how much you meant it—NO. I will not get hurt again. NO. I will not welcome anyone into my bed or my life. NO. I am not going to be vulnerable. Folks, I've said the same thing, and I've meant it. You draw a line in the sand and you absolutely mean it.

Until you don't.

So, if you want to take it back, that's okay. You should first be 100 percent over whoever your ex was. Be healed. Be okay with being single. Take a few months. Take a year. Take time to get your heart put together again. Take a breath.

Before you go onto the dating sites and looking for your person, tell the universe you're ready again.

Write yourself an email. Address it to your idea of God. Tell the universe that you appreciate the break from romance and that you're ready to try again.

Also tell it what you've learned from your last relationship. You know there's something. Whether it was a lesson about what worked or what didn't, it was important.

Say thank you for the time you've spent taking care of yourself. Promise not to lose that level of self-care when you meet someone. Hit send.

Find a quote that will help you remember how much you like yourself and how you're not willing to settle. Make that quote your screensaver on your phone.

FINDING LOVE

This love spell is about shifting your energy to be open to love. I have to say, you might not need this. Lots of folks go through life perfectly content without a partner.

SUPPLIES
Red or pink candle
Paper
Pen
Lighter
Fireproof dish
Red string or ribbon

Light the candle. On the left side of your piece of paper, write the qualities that you do not want in a partner, big things and little things. The little things often matter more than you think.

On the right side of your paper, write those qualities that you insist on in a partner. These things are non-negotiable. Here's an example:

They will not:	They will:
Make sockballs	Be kind
Cut corners	Be smart
Lie	Be funny
Break promises	Be silly
Make excuses	Be grounded most of the time
Be shy	Hold hands
Ask me for money	Enjoy sex
Have no self-esteem	Have a laugh that makes me
Be jealous	laugh
Sneakily pick their nose	Be brave
Make people feel small	Want to travel
	Love to read

Tear the paper in half. Burn the left side of the list and let the ashes blow away.

Fold the right side in half and in half again. On this side of the paper, write your intent: "I am looking for a partner." "I am looking for my person." "I am looking for fun."

Fold the paper again and tie the string around it.

Place the paper on or near the candle (please don't burn down your house) and visualize your partner.

The most important part of this spell happens afterward. When you go on dates, remember what was on that list. If it was important enough to put on the list, it's important enough to be non-negotiable. This is part of the list I made when I was looking for my person. I went on a lot of first dates afterward and was very aware of the other person's behavior. If they exhibited any of the left side, we were done. One guy snapped his fingers at a server. Yeah, we're done here. This is a competition for who is amazing enough to spend time with you. Make sure they earn your time.

Remember that dating is like trying on clothes to see what fits. If it doesn't fit, put it back. Do not DM back and forth for weeks before meeting. In doing that, you create a false relationship that exists between Fake Perfect You and Fake Perfect Them. Meet within a week or be done. Remember that your time is just as valuable as you are. Don't let the feeling in your stomach or your ego allow you to indulge in wasting time with people you're not really interested in or who are not a good match for you.

When I met my husband, I went home and checked the list. He met every single thing on it, except he hadn't watched *Doctor Who*. When I told him this, he binged it and finished it in a few weeks. So, I married him.

A WITCH BOTTLE FOR LOVE

Like the protection bottle, this is a little twist you can do with just as much intensity, for slightly sweeter rewards.

I know that a lot of love spells will encourage you to use a picture of the person you want to fall in love with you.

I think this is a terrible idea, and let me tell you why.

First, how do you know this person is not a total asshole? You don't. Second, they might not be willing to love you, so this is manipulative. Do you really want to be with someone who doesn't want to be with you? Last, consider the fact that if you choose a person to be in this spell for you, you are binding yourself with this person that, *yes*, makes your stomach and parts do that *thing*, but what if it doesn't work out? Now you have a bond with someone you might not even like anymore. Best to let those bonds develop naturally.

For this spell, we're going to tell the universe how we want to be treated. This isn't about finding a person directly. It's more about repelling those people who don't deserve your time.

SUPPLIES

Things that make you happy and represent love: rose quartz, flowers, perfume you love, honey, sugar, glitter, pine or cedar needles, scotch or whiskey, tiger's eye or jet, coffee

Jar or bottle with a lid that can seal

Red string

You're looking for things that make you comfortable. You want to put things in the jar that would draw good folks toward you. In the Harry Potter universe, there is a love spell called Amortentia that changes its scent for each person to whatever it is that attracts them. This is what we're going for. For example, mine would have cinnamon, vanilla, and nectarines.

As you prepare your spell and lay the ingredients in front of you, think of all the things that make you feel good. The touches, the words, the songs. Open yourself up to welcoming these things into your life.

Go to your quiet place. Imagine all the negative behavior you've received from people sliding off you. Imagine that you are receiving love, respect, and care. Stay here for a while.

Put your ingredients in the bottle. Seal the lid or stopper with wax.

Tie red string around the top and knot it three times.

Put the bottle under your bed.

After a year or so, you're going to want to find a new home for the bottle. This is because they tend to lose their efficacy after a while, and it's not a great idea to have a year's worth of intentions trapped in a bottle under your bed. You can bury it or re-cycle it.

I AM SHINY SPELL

This spell is to get you to fall more in love with yourself. Selfish isn't a bad thing. Selfish means that you put yourself first in life. This is the way it's supposed to be. As long as you aren't ignoring your obligation or treating other people like things, being selfish is actually healthy.

SUPPLIES

Pretty, nontoxic pen that you like (better if it has sparkles)
Picture of yourself. This should be a picture that you don't par-ticularly like. Maybe it was taken at an age when you were awkward. Maybe you were in a bad spot emotionally.
Long white ribbon
Oil for love

Go to your quiet place. With your pretty pen, write on your face. Write the things that you love about yourself. Write the nice things that you do. Write all the wishes that you've had granted, the good things that have happened to you, and the good things that you have done for other people. Write it all down until your face is covered with sparkly ink. As you're writing, recognize all the amazing things that you have done and will do. When you're finished, look at this sparkly piece of artwork that you've made. Look at the shiny piece of art that you *are*. Wrap the picture gen-tly with the white ribbon until it's completely obscured. Anoint it with any oil for love and then tuck it away on your altar or near your bed.

HEALING

I am a big fan of Eastern and Western medicine, and I would be the last person to tell you to rely on magic to heal yourself from illness. Science is a thing and it's important. However, I do think that your state of mind can help accelerate or decelerate healing. We have covered the psychology of magic in the first section of the book, but since medicine and magic seem counterintuitive, I wanted to revisit.

Back in the day, the wise women of the village were the healers. Before medicine became institutionalized and owned by the patriarchy, witches were healers. Part of the healing process is the balance between body, mind, and spirit. It is difficult to heal when your heart and soul are not in it. I was very ill for a really long time, and I'll tell you, as soon as I was well enough to feel even a tiny bit more optimistic, I seemed to improve quickly. Neuroplasticity allows the nerve cells in the brain to realign and compensate for injury and disease. It also reacts to changes in your environment and behavior patterns. Part of neuroplasticity is literally rewiring your brain into manifesting the results that you desire. This is not *The Secret*—you didn't get sick because you didn't want to be well enough. This is meditating and performing magic to get a better physical environment in which to improve your health.

With that said, please don't just do a magic spell and meditate and then wait for your pneumonia to clear up. Let's take the antibiotics *and* do magic and meditate.

SUPPLIES

Drink that makes you feel better
Blue candle

To perform this spell, you'll need peace and quiet for at least twenty minutes. Make your drink. My favorite thing is Moroccan mint tea with honey or throat coat tea. As you're making it, put care into the steps. Imagine the honey is glowing with a healing light. Imagine the hot water going to battle with the illness in your body.

Light your candle within your line of sight.

Sit down in a place where you can lie down. Stare at the candle and let your eyes go soft. Slowly drink your drink, imagining the whole time that the tea is winning the war against illness. As you drink it, picture a calm blue wave washing through your body and cooling off the fevers, washing away the illness.

When you've finished your drink, lie down and stare at the candle. Again, let your eyes go soft and imagine the light of the candle expanding and enveloping you. Picture the golden light sinking into your skin and meeting up with the blue wave on the inside.

Yellow and blue make green. Allow the two energies of water (tea) and fire (candle) to turn into a beautiful healing green and surround you.

Please go to sleep. It's good for you.

Try to do this whenever you lie down for a nap or go to bed. Keep drinking that tea or cocoa or water. Continue encouraging healing within and without. The key to this spell is to become an active participant in your own healing.

HEALING FOR OTHERS

Our world feels a little busted right now. Regardless of your political leanings, you need to see that the most vulnerable people in our communities are under intense pressure and danger. If you are doing well and have a position of privilege, you can use your magic to extend love, healing, and support. You can do this spell for a group of your friends, for a particular community, or for the whole world.

We're not trying to fix the world. We're going to give others some light so their path is safer. You have more power than you think you do, and doing spells like this can help your confidence in your magic grow, as well as share some sunshine with folks who need it.

It's super important to go into this magic with a clear mind. We're not sending hate to those who are threatening our folks. We're sending love, warmth, and visibility to the victims so that the oppressors aren't successful.

SUPPLIES
Permanent marker
2 orange seven-day or bodega candles
Picture or drawing of the community you're protecting
Matches

Go to your quiet place.

Write your gifts on the first candle. You have love, humor, fierce protectiveness, intelligence, stamina, rage … Write them down.

Write the receivers of your gifts on the second candle. Your family, the trans community, domestic violence survivors, the world.

On the picture of the community you're protecting, write the gifts that you wrote on the first candle. For example, "To the trans community. I bring my love, humor, protection, stamina, rage, and so on to you. I believe in you. I will stand with you."

Hold the first candle and look at the words that you've written. Own them. Light the candle with a match, then visualize the energy that you hold in your hands moving toward the community you want to protect.

Use the match to carry the flame from the first candle to the second. Focus on the picture of the community. Picture your gifts flowing out to the folks in that community. Picture the warmth and love enveloping them.

Place the picture underneath the second candle and let both candles burn together until they go out.

CELL PHONE MAGIC

Vision boards have taken on a whole new life since Oprah and *The Secret* mentioned them. A vision board is a collection of words and pictures that represent the future that you envision for yourself. On New Year's Eve, my family and I collect all the magazines that have accumulated over the year and cut them to pieces. Last year, my board had a crow with a pen in its mouth, a picture of Prince, a quote from Janelle Monáe, and the fortuitously phrased "Travel by Book." This year, that's exactly what I did. I went on a book tour with my kids, deepened my affinity for crows, and heard Prince and Janelle Monáe all the time. It's likely caused by the theory that when you are looking for connections, you're more likely to see them, but I think that that's a part of magic. You set the coding in your brain so that it can look for opportunities all around you. Gotta love neural plasticity.

You use your cell phone constantly, and sometimes to your own detriment. This spell is a great way to make it work *for* you. You can use this spell for lots of things, but here, we're going to set some goals related to love.

SUPPLIES

Cell phone

List of goals for the upcoming year

Stack of magazines

Glue sticks

¼ sheet poster board

Get comfy at your desk and piece together a collage of what you want your next year, month, or week to look like. Include words that resonate, flowers that make you happy, and people who embody traits you're striving for. You're creating your future, so set your goals high. I think people need to stretch to see what they're truly capable of. Include pictures of people you're attracted to, words like *passion* and *connection*, flowers that make you happy, and quotes that inspire you to not settle.

Take a screenshot or a snip of the collage and save it to your phone wallpaper and screensaver.

Every time you hold your phone, you'll see your dreams. You can even have a long-term collage for your background and a short-term goal for your screensaver. You're pushing forward your wishes and surrounding yourself with them all the time.

Make your phone work for you.

You can also set up reminders to set you on the path to your goals. If your goal is to work out three days a week, instead of putting hateful reminders on the phone or "work out, 5 p.m." three times a week, set random reminders about how strong you want to become. Set reminders with pictures of Linda Hamilton's arms or Pink's back muscles (Jesus Christ). Add some positivity to your goals.

RELEASING GRIEF

Holding on to grief can weigh you down needlessly. Of course, you should grieve the loss that you've experienced, but you can't live in it. After a while, it doesn't benefit you anymore. It no longer honors the person you lost. If you're feeling lonely, sad, rejected, or despairing, this spell can help. I've put it in the love chapter because there is no greater self-love than releasing those things that don't serve you.

SUPPLIES
Permanent marker
Small cloth
Stone (ideally rose quartz)
Plant or tree

You're going to send your grief into the ground. You're going to plant it and watch something beautiful grow from it. While you work, trace the timeline of your relationship with this person or circumstance in your mind, from the first day you met to the day you do the spell. If it helps, write this all down and include it in the packet. When I did this, I wrote my grandmother's name on a stone and buried it in a bereavement plant that I got from my workplace. Every time I see it, I think of her.

Write the name of what hurts you on the cloth. Wrap the stone in the cloth. Be gentle. This stone represents your heart.

Bury the stone and cloth under the plant or tree that you're planting.

This doesn't mean that you're going to have a symbol of your pain. This tree is going to be a testament to how strong you are and how much you can grow.

FEAR INTO ACTION

When you get frightened, you can freeze. Fear is important. It's part of your early warning system. It needs to be present, because the only folks who don't feel fear are toddlers and terrorists. Fear can keep you alive and keep you on solid footing in life. Sometimes, though, fear is a liability. Your beloved cat is sick and then feels better. They could be fine, sure, but maybe a trip to the vet is in order. The fear that something is terribly wrong can freeze you in your tracks. If you call the vet, you might lose your fuzzy friend. If you don't, they'll be okay for a while, right? Living in that gray space, with worry filling your mind every minute, is nearly as bad as finding out *why* they're sick. The what-ifs come out of every crevice in your mind, and the fear takes you away.

Whether it's taking your cat to the vet, calling about a bill that you know is late, or having a hard conversation, the fear of doing the thing can be worse than finding out the answer. This spell can help bridge that fear to get you past frozen.

SUPPLIES

Pen
Paper
Ziplock bag
Water
Salt
Eye protection
Hammer

First, go to your quiet place. Think of the worst things that can happen. Write them all down. Have a good cry if you need to. After you're finished, put the paper into a ziplock bag of water and salt, and toss it in the freezer. As you do this, imagine that all those possibilities are frozen. They're no longer options. This doesn't mean that they won't happen, just that they won't be hanging in your head while you're doing the hard thing.

Next, go do the thing. Remember that your anxieties are all frozen at home.

After you've completed the task, get the bag out of the freezer and take it outside. Go to someplace with a hard surface, put on your eye protection, and beat the living hell out of your anxieties with the hammer. Smash it until it's little tiny bits. Recycle the paper and walk away victorious.

Anxiety and fear are important, but they're not necessary, and they certainly don't get to tell you how to live your life.

☞ FOLK MAGIC AND SUPERSTITIONS FOR LOVE

Add some honey to food or drink for sweet conversations.

If the salt on the table is spilled, a quarrel among family members will happen before the day is through. Stop the quarrel by tossing some over your left shoulder.

My grandma Virginia would always say to lift your feet when you drive over railroad tracks, or you'll lose your love. I have no idea where this tradition comes from, but I do it anyway. Just in case.

Cinnamon across the thresholds and windowsills will bring love and health to the home.

Tourmaline kills jealousy.

Melting butter means love is in the room.

Use sugar to sweeten relationships.

CHAPTER 12
Divination

Divination is the practice of peeking a little further ahead so that you can make clear decisions. I always caution folks to not plan their lives around tarot cards. You still have to use common sense and realize that free will is a thing and that life changes pretty quickly. Divination is a tool. It's supposed to help you make decisions, not make decisions for you. With this in mind, it's a *really* cool tool. You can use forms of divination to help yourself and your friends and to keep yourself from dating doofuses. Divination can be an important part of magic, pointing you in the right direction before you start your spells. It can also help you create a timeline for events. When should I start looking for a new job? How long do I give my partner to change their behavior? This kind of magic works better when you can focus on when to do the work and when to expect the results.

CASTING CHARMS

Charms have been used forever for divination. I literally think it's been forever. Bones were some of the first charms used. Use feathers, shells, stones—whatever you can find and place meaning with. Our ancestors sought to obtain reason and knowledge from the world around them and decided that *this* stone meant that everything would be okay and that *that* stone meant it wouldn't be. Charms only need to have two things in order to be charms: they have to be small enough to cast (to throw down and read), and they have to mean something to you.

I started my charm collection with Carrie Paris's Magpie Oracle charms. This amazing part-fairy woman has curated several sets of charms to use for general reading, one for Lenormand readings, one for mediumship, and one for tarot. The kits are beautiful and are a wonderful way to start your own collection.

Bead stores are great for adding beads to your collection. So are walks. You can have a charm set that consists of only shells, each one holding a different meaning to you. You can collect stones, sticks, or bones. I think that adding to your charms as you get older makes it more meaningful to you. I have a set of yak knuckle bones that my friend Terry gave to me. They're special because of our friendship, how old they are, and how much use and love they've received. One of them is particularly special because my dog gnawed on it for a bit. Thanks a bunch, Lucy.

Once you've cobbled your charms together, you'll need a bag or a box to keep them in. I like using makeup bags and drawstring bags. You'll want something big enough that you can put your hand in and grab without seeing what you're getting. Be sure to keep the charms clean and in a safe place.

First, assign loose meanings to each of them. I say loose because a baby carriage charm for forty-five-year-old me who can't have more children would not mean the same to someone who was trying to start a family. For me, it might be the start of a new book or buying a new house.

You can use a casting cloth with assigned meanings to each section. You can also create a casting "cloth" by drawing a grid on a piece of paper. I don't use cloths or grids, preferring to get the meaning by the distance between the charms and which direction they're facing.

The questions you can ask your charms are endless. I usually just ask what's been on my mind the longest or what is currently irritating me the most.

Reach into your charm bag and pull out as many as feels right. Drop them over your casting area and see where they fall.

Pay attention to the way they're facing. How close are they in relation to each other? Does the meaning change when the ruler is next to the baby carriage? Perhaps this is telling you that precision is necessary with your new beginning.

I read the charms in a story. I start with the one closest to me and infer relationships between the charms that are near each other. Here's an example:

Question: What do I need to focus on right now?

Charms: Buddha head, dinner plate, book

Story: I need to relax and breathe, make sure I'm putting good things into my body, and do something that makes me happy.

I learned from Carrie that you can use your purse or pocket for charm casting. Decide what each item means and assign meaning to it. Keys mean yes, and lip balm means no. Rummage around in your bag. The one that you grab first is the answer to your question. This is a fantastic way to do divination in public without everyone being all up in your business.

BIBLIOMANCY

I have seven copies of the book *The Prophet* by Kahlil Gibran. I honestly have no idea why. I started purchasing them at book sales one at a time. I've never read this book all the way through. What I do instead is use the copies for bibliomancy. Interestingly, I've never used another book in this way.

Bibliomancy is the practice of using a book, often the Christian Bible, to perform divination. You think of or say a question, flip through the book to a random page, and put your finger down on the page. The passage that you land on is the answer to your question. It's undeniably creepy.

Recently, I was having a crappy day that was in reality only a crappy twenty minutes that I was allowing to pummel my perfectly normal day. I grabbed *The Prophet* and flipped to this: "You pray in your distress and in your need; would that you might pray also in the fullness of your joy and in your days of abundance."[21]

I was suddenly outside myself looking in. I have a home that I love, healthy kids, and a wonderful partner. I had twenty crap minutes and lost all perspective on my life. I was able to realign myself to what was actually going on and became calmer and refocused on what I was doing. And I had a better day.

Bibliomancy is helpful when you need an answer right away or if you've already tried other forms of divination that were not helpful. Sometimes, it's beneficial to let the universe talk while you listen.

---

21. Kahlil Gibran, *The Prophet* (New York: Knopf, 1968), 67.

PENDULUMS

There are so many ways to use a pendulum. You can purchase one made of crystal or stone; there is a list of magical qualities of stones on page 75. I like using jet (super grounding) and labradorite (enhances psychic energy). These can get a bit pricey, so if you can't swing it just now, you can use a ring on a string or a necklace with a pendant. The practice of divination using a pendulum is called pallomancy.

In a pinch, you can use your earbuds. Just be sure that the cord can swing freely from where you're holding it. I prefer using earbuds when I'm out in Muggle territory. Looks a lot less odd to be swinging an earbud around than to swing a rose quartz rock while holding it by the pewter fairy at the other end.

To perform pallomancy, go to your quiet, sacred space if you can. If you're in public, try to find some quiet.

Quiet your mind. Focus on your yes-or-no question. Hold the pendulum loosely.

Ask the pendulum (aloud or in your head), "Show me my yes." Generally, the pendulum will swing forward and backward. Then say, "Show me my no," and it will swing side to side.

Now you can ask your questions. Yes-or-no questions work the best, and diagonal swinging will indicate maybe.

You can use pendulum magic to ask anything. Will I get off work early today? Does she like me? Does she *like* like me?

I like to ask a few questions at first to make sure the pendulum is working with me that day. "Is my name Melissa?" "Am I fantastic?" Just those things that you know for certain.

There are a few things that you should be careful of. Don't overuse this. It can be really tempting to ask the same question over and over and over until you get the answer you want. This just causes anxiety and can trap you in a crazy question spiral.

Also, some folks can't use pendulums. My husband is like an energetic dead spot when it comes to pendulums. They'll swing for me and for everyone else in the room, and as soon as he touches them, they just stop. No movement at all. So odd.

You can also use pendulums to locate objects in a manner similar to dowsing. You can draw a map of the area where you've lost the item and move the pendulum over it slowly. When the pendulum starts moving, draw an enlarged version of the map that focuses on the part that got your pendulum swinging. In this fashion, you can narrow down a search from the whole house, to upstairs, to the living room, and then to the couch. It's remarkably accurate.

☛ RANDOM DIVINATION

Try a form of Polish divination: Blow out a candle three times. Smoke that flows up evenly predicts good health in the following year. If the smoke drifts around, it predicts illness or death.

If a broom falls, it means company is coming.

AUTOGRAPHY

There is a form of divination called autography, or automatic writing. You can do this with just a pen and some paper. My assumption is that my guides are the ones who are answering the questions I ask. It's hard to say, though, so if talking with spirits make you uncomfortable, you might want to skip this one.

In a relaxed state, ask a question either in your mind or out loud. You can start drawing loops or lines on the paper and then just let the writing go free. You should see some clear words that answer your question in the writing. Try to let your control go and just lean into the process of the automatic writing. This takes practice because we're so used to having complete control of our hands. It can lead to some pretty clear answers to pressing questions, though, so I encourage practice.

SCRYING AND CRYSTAL BALLS

Scrying is the act of divination in which you seek a vision by looking into an object. You can scry in any reflective surface, such as a bowl of still water, a mirror or piece of glass, a scrying stone (found in any new age shop), or a crystal ball.

I prefer to use crystal balls and candles. Again, it takes practice. Getting yourself into the proper mindset for scrying is a meditative practice, and you won't get much your first time out.

Light a small candle (votive or tea light) and place it on the opposite side of your crystal ball. You'll see the flame in the center of the crystal ball, inverted. Sit comfortably and relax your eyes so that the flame looks a little fuzzy. You can ask for signs or symbols verbally or in your mind, or you can just be still and see what the universe wants you to know. I always keep a notepad handy because for some reason, I'll see something and then it just leaves my mind. Super transient thoughts and ideas.

Be very careful to store your crystal ball out of direct sunlight. Not for any esoteric reason, but because if light hits it and reflects in a certain way, you can burn down your house. Also, if you drape it in a cloth, it's super dramatic when you unveil it, and you'll get witchy points.

TAROT

Tarot cards are a handy-dandy tool that you can use to look into the future. Also called cartomancy, this divination method was created sometime in the fourteenth century. Each deck has seventy-eight cards, composed of the major arcana and the minor arcana. The major arcana consists of twenty-two cards, and the minor arcana features fifty-six cards split into four suits: wands, cups, pentacles, and swords. The minor arcana has fourteen cards in each suit: one through ten, page, knight, queen, and king.

These cards help you focus your intuition. Again, like the pendulum, this is just a tool. You're the one with all the magic. I'm going to give you a super quick and dirty tarot lesson, but if you're interested in picking up the cards, there are some fantastic tarot books out there (*cough, cough* *Kitchen Table Tarot* *cough*).

First, choose a deck that you can work with and understand. Think of your question—yes-or-no questions aren't ideal for tarot. While you're thinking, shuffle the deck until you feel like you're ready. I always ask my clients to ask about what's worrying or exciting them the most.

After you're finished shuffling, cut the cards and stack them back up. Start with a three-card reading. The first card is the past, the middle is the present, and the right side is the future.

After placing the cards, you can look up the meanings in a book. For three-card readings, I recommend letting the cards tell you a story.

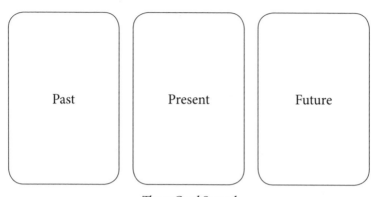

Three-Card Spread

Question: Should I continue with this job?

Cards: King of Swords, Page of Cups, Temperance

Your boss is kind of flinty, but your job is to bring comfort and calm to the office. If you can maintain your balance and not take his flintiness personally, you should be just fine.

Tarot Card Meanings

0. The Fool: I am going.
1. The Magician: I am doing.
2. The High Priestess: I am knowing.
3. The Empress: I am loving.
4. The Emperor: I am directing.
5. The Hierophant: I am unlocking.
6. The Lovers: I am focusing.
7. The Chariot: I am driving.
8. Justice: I am balancing.
9. The Hermit: I am thinking.

10. Wheel of Fortune: I am changing.

11. Strength: I am graceful.

12. The Hanged Man: I am releasing.

13. Death: I am weary.

14. Temperance: I am balancing.

15. The Devil: I am choosing.

16. The Tower: I am rebuilding.

17. The Star: I am hoping.

18. The Moon: I am wary.

19. The Sun: I am happy.

20. Judgement: I am seeing.

21. The World: I am transforming.

The Minor Arcana
The Aces: Essence

The aces are the very core of what the suits are. I've heard of spirit animals being called Bear or Fox, capital letters intending to put forth the idea that Fox is the essence of what it means to be a fox. It's the complete picture of what Fox entails—its traits, tendencies, everything. It is a generalization of what Fox is but paints a complete picture of the specific entity to which you are referring.

The aces are very similar, and they are the nucleus of each suit: the brain of the swords, the heart of the cups, the backbone of the wands, and the root of the pentacles. The traditional deck, the Rider-Waite-Smith, always makes me think of Monty Python, so I remember this because of the natural exaggeration of the tools. You've got the Hand of God bringing forth this wand or cup, and it's presented to you freely. The ace cards represent the pure, undiluted core of what that suit encompasses.

The Twos: Coming Together

The twos have a theme of plans coming together. The Two of Wands shows plans coming together before the action of the three. The cups are two people becoming a couple. The swords represent clarity of thought and ideas taking shape, and the pentacles show someone juggling all the responsibilities while their plans are flowing and taking shape beautifully.

The Threes: Journey

The threes represent a journey—an emotional, physical, or intellectual journey. What is certain about all four of the threes is that change is coming. The Empress is the third card of the major arcana. She's all about authenticity and relaxing into yourself. You can use that association to think about the threes in the minor arcana. The cards are about finding your stride and getting to the core of the issue, however painful or exhilarating that will be.

The Fours: Resting

In each of the fours, there is a moment of peace. Of grace, really. There's the awareness of your possessions and surroundings in the pentacles, the clarity of mind in the swords, the breath before the celebration in the wands, and even the weariness and ennui of the cups. There is a feeling of putting down defenses and relaxing into *now*. So much of tarot is looking to the future. The fours are present.

The Fives: Renewed Action

After the inertia of the fours, we're gearing up again. Pentacles represent recovery, cups regret, swords revenge, and wands revolt. The fives are about unrest and preparedness. These cards are hard. You don't get to pretty these up for clients; you have to just tell them what's going on. You can be optimistic with the fives and look to the next step, but you can't move on until you deal with the unrest and disruption that's going on.

The Sixes: Recognition

We look at the laurels that decorate the Six of Wands and then to the charity witnessed in the pentacles. We understand that we need to move forward to the safety that the swords urge us to, and the cups ask us to move backward into innocence. The sixes are all about recognition. Whether being recognized for your successes, seeing your place in the world, folding yester-you into present you, or finding a new home, the sixes want you to be aware of where you are, what you have around you, and what you need to do next. They are present-oriented cards.

The Sevens: Conflict

With the sevens, there is conflict. It ranges from conflicting ideals and morals to fighting or frustration. The sevens are not easy cards, especially if you're impatient. Each of the sevens says that you don't get what you want just yet. It doesn't matter how long you've wanted it, and it doesn't matter how close it appears to be. What matters is why you want it and how hard you will work for it.

The Eights: Hope

The eights are an interesting bunch. The pentacles are talking about hard work and investing in yourself for a better future, and the wands are similar, telling you to choose the best path and pour yourself into it. The cups and swords are fairly bleak, though. Where the first set is in the midst of hope and determination, the second two are occurring in the moment before the hope kicks in. There is still confusion, still unsurety, but the person is *this* close to getting that spark. Again, if we view the tarot cards as potentially kinetic, we look at what is actually happening in the reading. That moment when you raise your hand to be helped up. The moment when you decide it's time to go, pain or no. Those are the moments of time that keep our hearts lifted.

The Nines: Burgeoning

The nines are about maturing. Even the direst of the nines, the Nine of Swords, is about awareness. Awareness isn't always comfortable. It can make you see that your beloved relatives are bigots or that your marriage isn't always a marriage. Becoming aware is helpful in the cups for appreciating what you have, or in the pentacles for appreciating your harvest. The wands are waking you up to challenges to your moral core. When you grow up, your values change and your perception shifts. It's important to grow along with those changes, or we run into trouble. The nines are essentially about becoming awake to the world around you—to the present. It's a wonderful thing.

The Tens: Excess

The tens are just overdone. So much. How flipping long can you stand and wave at a rainbow? What happens after that? I've been thinking a lot lately about self-differentiation. My minister gave a wonderful sermon about it, and it stuck in my head and has been bouncing around for quite a while. My friend Susan asked me after the service to tell her "something about tarot" and I blurted out, "The tens! The tens are all about having a poorly differentiated self and carrying around other people's nonsense and drama…" and then I think I started staring off into the distance and muttering to myself.

You can be empathetic without owning someone else's tragedy. You can be compassionate without carrying their hurt around with you. You can cause people to be disappointed because you act one way and not another, and you can be okay with that disappointment. You can learn to listen to someone's anxiety without being anxious yourself, and you can absolutely hear "It's not you, it's me" and believe it.

So the tens—they're a lot. A lot more than people need, for sure.

Pages: The Id

The pages are the noobs of the court cards. They're learning and exploring and likely are going to drop their tools on their way to mastery. This is okay, though. That's what you're supposed to do when you're learning. You watch other people; you pick up their habits and then you make them your own. The pages are experimenting with who they want to be. They're figuring out how to move in the world and will often make mistakes—just like all of us.

Knights: The Ego

The knights are midway to mastery. They are arrogant and full of beans, so to speak, and they aren't overly concerned about other people's needs or expectations of them. The knights are task oriented and self-oriented and are going to get things done. The details are often up in the air and up for ignoring completely. They're on their way to being the kings but aren't quite there yet.

Kings: The Superego

The kings are knowledgeable, right, and absolutely sure of their rightness. They have been through all the stages of learning and have settled into their wealth of information comfortably. They won't be shifted by your wants, needs, or concerns, unless it affects the greater good. The greater good is completely subjective depending on their goals. Maddening but important. Someone has to make those decisions. Someone has to be right.

Queens: The Heart

The queens are the chewy emotional center of the tarot. They are the heart and the feelings and the emotional base of the court cards. They can be cold or engaged, withdrawn or supportive. Basically, if you think of every trope that the word *mother* encapsulates, this is the queens. You can read into their elements to see how they will interact with you and how the cards will play in your reading. Queen of Cups? Love and support. Queen of Swords? A critical eye and approach.

Cleansing Your Cards

After some use, your cards will get energetically funky. You can reset the energy a few ways.

- Put the cards in order in each suit, and then put the major arcana in order as well.

- Use incense or sage to clean the cards with smoke.

- Give them a break. Put them on your altar with a crystal or stone on top. Selenite is great for this.

- Rap on the top of them three times with your knuckles.

FOLK MAGIC AND SUPERSTITIONS: DIVINATION IS FOR THE BIRDS

Crows carry the neighborhood news. If you leave unsalted peanuts out for the crows, they might bring you gifts as well.

A mated pair of cardinals in a tree on your property means your home is healthy and loving.

Cardinals can also mean that you're being visited by a loved one who has crossed over.

Blue jays in the yard mean quarrels among inhabitants of the house. Blue jays are generally the assholes of the bird world, so this checks out.

Hawks carry messages from the spirit world. If a loved one who has passed comes to mind when you see one, they are with you.

If you see a bird in your house, it means that love will fly away.

If you find a good parking spot, you'll have a good shopping trip. If you can't find a parking spot, say, "Blackfeather, blackfeather, please help us land." You'll find one within minutes. Don't forget to say thank you.

If you see a heron, it foretells good luck.

Seeing eggshells on the ground is a sign of change coming your way.

Counting magpies and crows is an old form of divination.

Count the number you see in a gathering, and the number means this:

One for sorrow
Two for joy
Three for a girl
Four for a boy
Five for silver
Six for gold
Seven for a secret
Never to be told
Eight for a wish
Nine for a kiss
Ten for a bird
You must not miss

Conclusion

What do you do now? You've got a handful of spells and some guidelines to your magical self, life, and tools. The next step is to either create your own magical practice or reach out to your community to further refine and expand your magical world. Read more books. Find a way to tie the magic you've learned to your spirituality. Practice. Keep a journal of what works and what doesn't.

You don't have to reach out to build a magical community if you don't want to. My magic has been private for most of my life. When I *do* get together with my fellow witches, it's because I trust them implicitly. I've spent time with them and know them as people. If I know that you have good ethics and a moral compass that points about the same way mine does, I will do magic with you. Don't be too free with your hearts. Remember that folks have to earn your trust.

In your life, you have run into magic 100 times in 100 different ways. You have felt its effect and your body, mind, and soul have been aware of its energy. I hope that this book will help you own the magic you have and tap into the magic that you are surrounded by. There are so many wonderful magical books out there that I was a little daunted at the undertaking. I was heartened by the fact that not many of them hand you straight magic without religion. I don't want anyone to be intimidated away from magic. It's our birthright.

I wrote *Kitchen Table Magic* for the same reason that I wrote *Kitchen Table Tarot*: I wanted people to stop feeling intimidated by tools and traditions that can make their lives better. Magic will make you powerful, and tarot is an amazing tool to help you succeed in life. These reasons alone are enough for folks to have made both practices "secret" or "sacred" and out of your reach. Don't let anyone limit your access to something that already belongs to you. My magic has always been a personal, private thing that has only been shared with my loved ones. Enough of that. Let's come out of the broom closet together.

You can also just connect with other magic people online. There is no reason to put yourself in jeopardy of losing your job or friends or family. There is no reason to share your personal practices when you don't feel comfortable. Use a different name, like Linnea Ravensbane, and reach out to people to learn more about magic without putting yourself in anxious waters.

These gifts are yours as much as your hearing or sight or sense of taste belongs to you. How you use magic is up to you. I hope that you have as much joy with it as I do. Since I've pulled magic into the front of my life instead of the cupboard, I have felt calmer, more in control, and less likely to fear anything that might come at me.

Remember that your magic is yours and that it can manifest in whatever way you'd like. You can pair it with your spiritual tradition to forge a closer relationship to your idea of deity, or you can make it a part of your political activism. You can use magic to enhance your sex life and to become a better partner or friend.

I hope that pulling your magic out into the open makes you feel more empowered. Sometimes I forget that I'm a witch. Things go sideways and then, in a moment of sadness, I remember my tools. I can write a petition to the universe. I can meditate. I can light a candle. I can decide the shape of my life and push it in the right direction. I can bring clarity to my problems with the light of one candle.

I hope you feel the same way and that your magic spreads and takes on the shape and sense of your life. Make it your own. Take these seeds that I've handed you and go build a garden of wonder and badassery.

XOXO,
Melissa

Recommended Reading List

MAGIC

Inner Witch by Gabriela Herstick
High Magick by Damien Echols
Six Ways by Aidan Wachter
Making Magic by Briana Saussey

TAROT

Anything by Mary K. Greer and Rachel Pollack
Queering the Tarot by Cassandra Snow
Tarot for One by Courtney Weber
Going Beyond the Little White Book by Liz Worth
Tarot Inspired Life by Jaymi Elford

ASTROLOGY

Astrology for Real Life by Theresa Reed
Astrology for Happiness and Success by Mecca Woods
Magickal Astrology by Skye Alexander
You Were Born for This: Astrology for Radical Self-Acceptance by
    Chani Nicholas

Bibliography

Adler, Margot. *Drawing Down the Moon.* New York: Viking Press, 1979.

Bible. King James 2000 Version. Edited by Robert A. Couric. Self-published, 2000.

B., Margi. "Polish Folk Magic." Letters of Lilith. 2003. http://lilithgate.atspace.org/articles/magic.html.

Bowes, Sue. *Woman's Magic.* Newburyport, MA: Weiser Books, 1999.

Cantrell, Gary. *Wiccan Beliefs and Practices.* St. Paul, MN: Llewellyn Publications, 2001.

Carney, Dana R., Amy J. C. Cuddy, and Andy J. Wap. "Power Posing: Brief Nonverbal Displays Affect Neuroendocrine Levels and Risk Tolerance." *Psychological Science* 21, no. 10 (2010): 1363–68. doi:10.1177/0956797610383437.

Doty, James. *Into the Magic Shop: A Neurosurgeon's True Story of the Life-Changing Magic of Compassion and Mindfulness.* London: Yellow Kite, 2016.

Fogg, Kiera. *Crystal Gridwork*. Newburyport, MA: Weiser Books, 2018.

Gibran, Kahlil. *The Prophet*. New York: Knopf, 1968.

Gladwell, Malcolm. *Blink*. New York: Little, Brown, 2005.

Hodorowicz Knab, Sophie. *Polish Customs, Traditions, and Folklore*. New York: Hippocrene Books, 1993.

Hubbard, Bethany. "Your Bacterial 'Aura' Follows You from Place to Place." *Discover*, August 28, 2014. https://www .discovermagazine.com/health/your-bacterial-aura-follows -you-from-place-to-place#.VAEj4GSSy61.

Jackowski, Karol. *Sister Karol's Book of Spells, Blessings, and Folk Magic*. Newburyport, MA: Weiser Books, 2019.

Mangan, James Clarence. "St. Patrick's Hymn before Tarah." In *Library of the World's Best Literature*. Vol. 17. Edited by Charles Dudley Warner. New York: The International Society, 1897. https://www.bartleby.com/library/poem/3415.html.

McCabe, Ian. *Carl Jung and Alcoholics Anonymous*. London: Routledge, 2015.

McCammon, Robert. *Boy's Life*. New York: Simon & Schuster, 1992.

McKechnie, Sam, and Alexandrine Portelli. *The Magpie & the Wardrobe: A Curiosity of Folklore, Magic & Spells*. London: Pavilion Books, 2015.

Nemeth, Maria. *The Energy of Money: A Spiritual Guide to Financial and Personal Fulfillment*. New York: Ballantine, 1997.

Robbins, Tom. *Even Cowgirls Get the Blues*. New York: Bantam Dell, 1976.

Saussy, Briana. "How to Make a Honey Jar (with Pictures!!!)." BrianaSaussy.com. Accessed February 25, 2020. https://briana saussy.com/how-to-make-a-honey-jar-with-pictures/.

Schur, Michael, dir. *Parks and Recreation*. Season 4, episode 16, "Sweet Sixteen." Aired February 23, 2012, on NBC. https:// www.hulu.com/series/parks-and-recreation-93dc18da-96d9 -4841-b125-40f901f7e7eb.

Scott, Sabrina. *Witchbody*. Newburyport, MA: Weiser Books, 2019.

Starhawk. *Truth or Dare: Encounters with Power, Authority, and Mystery*. New York: HarperCollins, 1987.

Wachter, Aidan. *Six Ways*. New Mexico: Red Temple Press, 2018.

White, Gregory Lee. *The Use of Magical Oils in Hoodoo, Prayer, and Spellwork*. Nashville, TN: White Willow Books, 2017.

TO WRITE TO THE AUTHOR

If you wish to contact the author or would like more information about this book, please write to the author in care of Llewellyn Worldwide Ltd. and we will forward your request. Both the author and publisher appreciate hearing from you and learning of your enjoyment of this book and how it has helped you. Llewellyn Worldwide Ltd. cannot guarantee that every letter written to the author can be answered, but all will be forwarded. Please write to:

Melissa Cynova
℅ Llewellyn Worldwide
2143 Wooddale Drive
Woodbury, MN 55125-2989

Please enclose a self-addressed stamped envelope for reply,
or $1.00 to cover costs. If outside the U.S.A., enclose
an international postal reply coupon.

Many of Llewellyn's authors have websites with additional information and resources. For more information, please visit our website at http://www.llewellyn.com